NO PLACE TO GO

HOW PUBLIC TOILETS FAIL OUR PRIVATE NEEDS

LEZLIE LOWE

COACH HOUSE BOOKS, TORONTO

first edition

 Canada Council   Conseil des Arts
for the Arts   du Canada

 ONTARIO ARTS COUNCIL
CONSEIL DES ARTS DE L'ONTARIO
an Ontario government agency
un organisme du gouvernement de l'Ontario

Canadä

Published with the generous assistance of the Canada Council for the Arts and
the Ontario Arts Council. Coach House Books also acknowledges the support
of the Government of Canada through the Canada Book Fund and the Government of Ontario through the Ontario Book Publishing Tax Credit.

LIBRARY AND ARCHIVES CANADA CATALOGUING IN PUBLICATION

Lowe, Lezlie, 1972-, author
    No place to go : how public toilets fail our private needs / Lezlie Lowe.

Issued in print and electronic formats.
ISBN 978-1-55245-370-4 (softcover).--ISBN 978-1-77056-561-6 (EPUB).--
ISBN 978-1-77056-562-3 (PDF)

    1. Public toilets--Social aspects. 2. Restrooms--Social aspects. I. Title.

GT476.L69 2018   392.3'6   C2018-903922-1
                                                             C2018-903923-X

No Place To Go is available as an ebook: ISBN 978 1 77056 561 6 (EPUB) ISBN
978 1 77056 562 3 (PDF)

Purchase of the print version of this book entitles you to a free digital copy. To
claim your ebook of this title, please email sales@chbooks.com with proof of
purchase. (Coach House Books reserves the right to terminate the free digital
download offer at any time.)

*For Lily and Georgia, whose early
urban adventures started this whole thing*

1

GAME OF THRONES

Spring 2005. I abandon my kids and trundle down the grimy concrete stairs to the public bathrooms in the bunker-like Pavilion on the Halifax Common. Practically every day – summer, fall, spring, and winter, doesn't matter – I yank on the heavy door, more surprised when it budges than when it doesn't. Getting in is only something of an advantage. These public bathrooms are smelly and soap-free. There's no changing table, often no paper towels, and the hand dryers have been smashed off the walls. I turn around and climb the stairs to retrieve my girls. To use these city-run facilities, I leave my double stroller and the rest of my belongings outside, crossing my fingers that nothing gets stolen while I help a toddler down the stairs, balancing an infant and lugging a diaper bag.

I brave it. My bladder's weak, always has been. It's not a medical condition. It's just that, when I have to go, I *really* have to go. What's more, my feeble ability to hold it far exceeds my toilet-training three-year-old's, so daily down the stairs I tromp to give that handle a yank. Most days, it's no go, which means a quick turnaround to head home to pee or change someone's pants. I'll learn later that the softball league that uses the diamonds on weekends has copies of the keys; they turn the deadbolts when they leave on Sunday evenings, lest up-to-no-good mothers like me get in and mess up the place.

I'm on the Common because it's close to my home: a convenient place to go to get the heck out of the house. Being free of four walls with young kids is a prophylactic against maternal madness, and the Halifax Common is a central park on downtown's edge with plenty of grass and trees, and paths for strolling. The Common was set aside in 1749 as a community livestock pasture (the irony here is inescapable – this place was, at one time, a giant bathroom). Having banished sheep and cows, the modern Common's twelve hectares hold tennis courts, ball diamonds, a skate park, a swimming pool, and a splash pad. The place is built for leisure. Unless, that is, you're the kind of person who uses the bathroom.

Every time I'm out with my infant and toddler, I need to change a diaper or respond to the urinary urgency of my toileter-to-be. Often both. Every time. Parents reading this know it to be true. So it's inconceivable – though here I am living it – that no municipal workers seem to check that the Common bathrooms are open, let alone clean and stocked. This is simply what passes for a public toilet in Halifax, Nova Scotia, in 2005. And, look, that's no slag on my home city. Halifax is a provincial capital and regional centre with six universities, active arts and sports scenes, and access to the unbounded wild within a thirty-minute drive of downtown. In short: we take quality of life seriously. This same kind of sad-excuse-for-a-public-toilet is what passes in cities and parks all over North America even today.

And this, precisely, is the problem.

It's the reason I carry little girls' underwear in my purse. It's the reason I've developed toilet radar; the reason the first thing I look for in a new environment is the closest place to pee. It's the reason I started to ask questions about public toilets. Like, why aren't there more of them, in a developed country with enough money to fund polar and space exploration and to give generous tax breaks to multinational corporations? And how is it that, with kids, I started having so much trouble navigating a city that I used to steer through relatively problem-free? People tell you your life changes once you become a parent. And it's true: I sure started seeing public bathrooms differently.

Or, you might say I started seeing them at all. And once I began to think about toilets, I couldn't stop. The more I learned, the more it struck me that the history of public toilets in cities is the history of cities themselves. Toilets have been a central, recurring theme in my journalism practice ever since I wrote my very first piece as a staff writer for Halifax's alternative weekly paper, the *Coast* (that's when I found out the softball leagues were the ones locking me out). Public bathrooms are invariably one of the highlights (or lowlights) of my travels. My holiday pics are flooded with public-bathroom shots; I reach excitedly for my Twitter feed when I find a great bathroom sign, like the ones at Edinburgh's Meadows park, which include distances along with way-finding. Public bathrooms, so seemingly mundane, keep me up at night. They spell out how unwillingly we share public space, how we would rather pretend we never defecate or urinate (or, for that matter, menstruate). Public bathrooms are private spaces that reveal public truths. I can't help myself. I have to peek inside.

My bathroom fiascos on the Halifax Common aren't just my stories; they are the province of parents all over. For most North American kids, the leap out of diapers happens around age three. Toilet training is a time of frayed nerves, when leaving the house goes high-stakes. Kids – non-parents may be unaware here – give little warning of impending sanitary disaster. It can be zero to puddle in under sixty. And in the miraculous case that a new underpantser is aware enough to give the gotta-go in time, a most pressing question indeed presents itself: where?

I call Andreae Callanan, a friend of a friend in St. John's, Newfoundland. I want the perspective of a parent in a different city, and one with higher stakes. Callanan has four kids. She knows this game of thrones. 'I can't even think of how many times my children have had to pee in an alleyway or behind a bush, or a mailbox,' she says. 'You do these things because you have to.' This isn't dinner-party conversation. No parent wants to explain that his kid pooped on the playground slide, or describe how he cleaned it up with a McChicken container fished out of the trash. Callanan tells me she once changed a soiled diaper in an outhouse-sized café bathroom in Montreal, aiming a soggy child into a clean diaper balanced on her lap as the then-new mom sat on a toilet. The nanny of one of my friends is horrified at the lack of public bathrooms in parks in her adopted city of Ottawa. She's taught her three-year-old charge to pee on the back of the electrical box at one of the parks. 'I wasn't sure if that was an attempt at privacy,' my friend confides, 'or a passive "fuck you" to the Parks and Rec department.'

Employing the electrical-box fix or not, parents and caregivers of children, especially those in the throes of toilet training, must develop an expertly tuned bathroom homing device. For Callanan, downtown St. John's presents an Ancient Mariner–calibre conundrum – bathrooms, bathrooms everywhere, but not a place to pee. Think about it: every commercial building has a bathroom. Every café and store, and restaurant. Ditto for office towers and government buildings, which Callanan eyes directly. 'These are companies with gazillions of dollars. They already have staff to keep the building clean, and they can't have this little bit of generosity to open up two clean rooms? It just seems so stingy.' It's not that simple, of course. Provision costs. There's add-on water and paper, and electricity. Extra cleaning. Perhaps more significantly, providing bathrooms means welcoming the world and being okay with it. There's an element of people – unhoused people, drug dealers or drug users, those cruising for sex or looking for a place to nap – that businesses usually want to keep out, and that goes even if those folks only want to come in to actually use the bathroom. Keeping some out is most easily achieved by keeping everyone out.

Callanan goes to the park with her kids regularly from about March through December. But almost all St. John's park bathrooms – there are about fourteen across the metropolitan area to serve 200,000 people – are open Victoria Day in May through Labour Day. After that, parks staffing is cut back because kids are in school, days are getting shorter, and temperatures are dipping. 'We generally only have walkers then,' says St. John's deputy city manager Paul Mackey when I speak to him in the fall of 2014. 'Not so much activity.' So for Callanan (and presumably all those lonely walkers), it's the bushes.

The St. John's Parks and Open Spaces Master Plan was presented to city council in late 2014. The plan was the result of scads of public meetings, but the records of the consultation include no mention of bathrooms whatsoever. Mackey tells me toilets weren't part of the discussion because that would have been going into too high a level of detail. But, he says, the city has heard an earful from walkers on the Grand Concourse portion of the Newfoundland T'Railway, who wonder where they're supposed to find relief along the pathway's nearly two hundred kilometres. The Grand Concourse was designed to encourage active transportation and links St. John's with eight-and-counting bedroom communities. Mackey says it's well-used. 'In the winter, people are still walking.' (Mackey himself may now have joined them; he retired in 2015.) Some others, like Callanan, are out playing in the snow with their kids. Contrary to the point of urban parks, sometimes she opts for the mall when she needs to get everybody out of the house. It's a 'much less stimulating but accessible environment,' she says. She would rather spend her money downtown, but at times the burden of being on bathroom red alert is too tiring.

It's easy to pretend public bathrooms don't need any fixing when no one talks reasonably about their problems. Toilet talk boomerangs between clinical and bust-a-gut. We can spill to our doctors about our toilet habits. (Well, some of us, anyway.) We can toss out potty jokes. But we don't have the language to deal with the everyday. Your kid had to squat behind a shrub and wipe with purse-bottom-mottled Kleenex? You shit your pants in line at Starbucks because you had to buy something to get a bathroom key? Or at Tim Hortons, because you'd been denied the key due to some prior misdeeds. (For context on this one, search Google videos for some combination of 'Tim Hortons,' 'British Columbia,' and 'angry pooper.' Actually, you know what? Don't.) *La-la-la... I can't hear you...* Meanwhile, targeted ads follow us around the internet pushing plush toilet paper and wet wipes. The glossy design mags I browse at my local magazine store paint clean scenes of fluffy towels and svelte toilets looking more like hat boxes than your average commode. It's not difficult to see where the bathroom-sexiness line is drawn. Toilet advertising is all about improving the private bathroom experience selling luxury, cost-saving eco-friendliness, or hypercool design. It's not about bettering public conveniences and simple access. After all, what's there to sell in a public bathroom? There's no commerce in social justice and public health.

Plus, on a global scale, we've got it good. Here's a truth bomb, care of the World Health Organization (who) and United Nations

Children's Fund (UNICEF): 2.3 billion people live without basic sanitation – roughly equivalent to the populations of Africa, North America, and Southeast Asia *combined*. That count is from the 2017 sustainable development goals *Progress on Drinking Water, Sanitation and Hygiene*. And, while the report acknowledges that things are getting better, the goal of universal basic sanitation by 2030 will not be met at the current rate of improvement.

One solution, such as it is, for lack of basic sanitation is open defecation, which I'm sorry to say is exactly what you're likely picturing – people shitting in fields and on streets. Open defecation is a daily reality for 892 million people, most of them in Central and Southern Asia and sub-Saharan Africa. Inadequate sanitation and open defecation spread disease – intestinal worms, schistosomiasis, and trachoma, for starters – and causes diarrhea, which is directly responsible for the deaths of 280,000 people a year, according to the WHO and UNICEF. Add in the related woes of inadequate water and hygiene, and the number of annual deaths shoots to 842,000. Almost half are children under five.

Take a second to sit with that. Almost half the deaths are of infants and toddlers. When a child in Halifax gets diarrhea, she goes to bed, rests up, and maybe munches some pediatric electrolyte freeze-pops. In too many nations, diarrhea, added to a lack of easy access to clean drinking water, soap, and a place for handwashing, mows down 361,000 little kids a year, plus another 480,000-odd adults. These are staggering numbers, and ones, perhaps, easy to dismiss as you fill a water bottle at your kitchen sink. But know this: open defecation happens in major North American cities, too. When homeless people look too shabby to be welcome in cafés and malls, when they're unsheltered and sleeping rough, when they don't have a free on-street bathroom to visit, or enough spare change to pump into one of the automatic public toilets (APTs) spouting like mushrooms in some North

American cities, they have to go somewhere. The average person goes to the bathroom six to eight times a day. You do the math.

Spring 2014. The never-open Pavilion public bathrooms of my kids' childhoods are now caged with chain-link and permanently padlocked. Those dank concrete stairs I used to clunk down now collect desiccated leaves and McDonald's coffee cups. The city will open them for special events if organizers put in a request, but I can't fathom they're used much. Halifax's supervisor of contract services, John Cook, takes me in to show me around. The bathrooms are ghostly and dark, and notably cleaner than I've ever seen them. The chipped plywood stalls have been replaced with plastic laminate separators, the broken mirrors removed. Still, no strollers or wheelchairs can get in, and even for the able-bodied who can get down the stairs, there's something eerie about this windowless, subterranean space. It feels, from the perspective of a woman, too easy to be trapped, too difficult to be heard. Most people probably make the two-minute walk to the new public washrooms on the other side of the Common, even when these are open.

The new bathrooms were built in 2007 in response to the community clamouring for better provision. Business owners were fed up with people asking to use their customer washrooms because the Pavilion toilets were dirty, scary, or locked. A nearby Royal Canadian Legion reported to the city that, on average, three hundred people a day were coming through the door to relieve themselves. The new Common bathrooms are large, accessible, and, crucially, more vandalism-proof than those of the Pavilion, which was racking up somewhere in the range of $30,000 for annual fix-ups, graffiti removal, and repainting. But vandal-proofing comes at a different cost. At the new Common bathrooms, there are no mirrors at the sinks and no paper towels. The taps, flushers, and hand dryers are automatic. This provokes uneasy, perhaps unanswerable, questions: What makes a good public bathroom? Can durability go too far? I appreciate the new Common bathrooms, I do. But, jeez, there aren't even toilet seats. You just perch on a cold stainless-steel rim.

I get it – unbreakability is a virtue. These are public bucks and taxpayers are tight-fisted hands at the grindstone. But the new Common bathrooms don't necessarily address user needs. They're open only 8 a.m. to 10 p.m., which sticks early-morning exercisers or anyone walking across the Common late at night (it's a popular route from downtown bars to Halifax's west-end and university neighbourhoods) back in the bushes. Plus, when the city built this brick shithouse, it didn't winterize it. The bathrooms are closed November 1 through May 1, recalling downtown St. John's – though there, according to Paul Mackey, most of the bathrooms are winterized; it's just that there's little winter demand. In Halifax, it's a perplexingly opposite situation – great demand and no ability to open the bathrooms. The Halifax Common has become a winter hot spot since the addition of a four-hundred-metre speed-skating oval in 2010. The oval sees more than 120,000 skaters through December, January, February, and March. Within a year of its opening, the city installed a brick plaza, a special events stage, a warming trailer, and a massive piece of public art. As far as bathrooms? The city brought in a row of porta-potties. There are no signs on the Common, or the surrounding area, to light the way for toilet seekers. Unless you know where you're going, you're not going at all. Stand in the middle of the Common and punch 'public washroom' into Google Maps and all you get is a single hit: a bathroom on the waterfront that's a twenty-one-minute walk away.

The ramifications here seem clear, not least for tourism. Holidaymakers who don't have to rush back to their hotels are more likely to stay out and spend money. In most respects, Halifax is pretty savvy when it comes to catering to its 5.3 million annual overnight visitors. And why wouldn't it be attentive to an industry that, in 2017, pumped $1 billion into the city's economy? Yet showing the way to the city's paltry flushable resources isn't a priority for Halifax's tourism marketing agency, Destination Halifax, because, apparently, no one ever mentions it to them. When I began researching this book in 2014, I was told they'd never had a single complaint about the dearth of signs (or public toilets). 'It sounds like one of those things,' then city spokesperson Shaune MacKinlay told me, 'that nobody has given a lot of thought to.' You don't say?

Perhaps the issue deserves an ear. A string of small communities in the British Columbia interior began focusing on public bathroom installation in 2017 as a way to boost tourism; ditto Denver, Colorado, which introduced two mobile public facilities the same year. If Nova Scotia hopes to hit its goal of $4 billion in annual tourism revenue by 2024, led by its capital city, it will likely be flush in more ways than one.

Speaking of tourism, Lunenburg, Nova Scotia, makes a perfect day trip from Halifax. It's also a good little town to have a pee in. The UNESCO World Heritage Site was founded in 1753 and today is peppered with colourful wood-shingled houses and shops, and prominent kiosk signs listing the town's main attractions, like the Fisheries Museum of the Atlantic, the rebuilt schooner *Bluenose II*, and the town's kick-ass stand-alone public bathroom. 'We are a community that actively seeks tourist traffic,' says Mayor Rachel Bailey. 'A washroom is kind of a necessity.' And that was the very moment I fell in love with Mayor Bailey.

The Lunenburg public bathroom opened in 2001 and was designed to emulate a Lunenburg cape-style home from the 1700s. It's the only stand-alone public washroom in town, but Lunenburg is small (2016 population: 2,263) – it's the kind of place where a real, live human answers when you ring the main municipal line – and the bathroom is easy to get to even from the farthest reaches of the town centre. Mayor Bailey nevertheless suggests Lunenburg could do better, commenting that the north and east ends of town are not as well served as the bathroom-boasting west. Bailey is unswayed when I point out how short that distance is – even a hyperbolist couldn't estimate the distance across Lunenburg's downtown as more than a kilometre. 'I know when you have little ones,' she says, 'you don't always have a lot of time to make it.' (Preach, Mayor Bailey, preach!) There's long been talk of adding a second permanent public washroom, and the town's waterfront development agency is working on plans for bathroom and shower facilities at the other end of the boardwalk. In the meantime, Lunenburg has porta-potties in areas where there are more people and more need, and the town is actively working to make its existing bathrooms accessible to the public, like the one at town hall, which is not accessible, but clean, well-stocked, and very well signed.

The design of the little clapboard Lunenburg public washroom is not the stuff of afterthought. It's on a main street – Bailey: 'That's where the people are' – and fits puzzle-like into the town's architecture. Outside the building are a bench, a stone terrace, and, in season, an abundance of columbines and hostas. The interior boasts painted tiles created by one hundred elementary school students who walked the streets of their town choosing flowers, houses, sailboats, and cats to render for the bathroom, each tile its own scene. The bathroom art has been made into a series of cards sold by the Lunenburg Heritage Society. Bea Renton, Lunenburg's chief administrative officer, tells me she gets emails from tourists in praise of the toilets.

Lunenburgers paid just over $100,000 to build their bathroom and they shell out a little over $14,000 a year to operate and maintain it during its open season, from mid-May through Halloween.

It used to close in mid-October, but council voted to extend the dates based on requests from residents and will keep it open later depending on the weather and the need. Opening it all winter is an option, Bailey says, based on demand. The town can also take in revenue from the bathroom by renting space in the front lobby.

I caught wind of the Lunenburg toilet from a friend who stumbled upon it and emailed me a report: 'Lunenburg has an outstanding public washroom,' she told me. 'In a cool building near the waterfront.' She noted it was spacious and clean and blended into its surroundings. My friends know me well (as does my husband, who snaps pics of 'Customers Only' bathroom signs and texts them to me, anticipating my outrage). They're used to my reporting, both social and professional, and my non-stop touring of the public bathrooms I encounter, whatever city I happen to be in. Like I said, I can't help myself. The public toilet is a peephole into our public and private selves.

Barbara Penner is a senior lecturer in architectural history at London's Bartlett School of Architecture and the author of 2014's *Bathroom*. In these seemingly mundane spaces, Penner says, 'you quite quickly understand what society thinks is important.' Those who are closest to me – and even those who aren't – invariably laugh at my abiding obsession with public bathrooms. That's fine with me. And with Penner. 'People's initial response is often, "Hee hee hee,"' she tells me over Skype from her London office, 'but followed quite often by very personal confessions.' After all, we all have a personal relationship with public toilets. They are as inescapable as our desire to leave our homes, as unavoidable as the human need to urinate and defecate. As author Rose George writes in *The Big Necessity: The Unmentionable World of Human Waste and Why It Matters*, 'To be uninterested in the public toilet is to be uninterested in life.' So? What are we waiting for? Let's go.

2

WAITING FOR A MIRACLE

I have spent my lifetime waiting in toilet lines. Leaning on the wall, staring at the floor, fiddling with my phone, or making idle chitchat with my neighbours in the queue. I grew up being socialized to expect a line for the bathroom. I spent decades so desensitized to the indignity that I never questioned it. Once, as a child, I peed my pants waiting in a bathroom line at a community hall dance. All the while, the boys' bathroom door hung ajar, the light on, the room unoccupied. I could literally *see* the toilet. Not a single girl in that line made a move.

I filed that experience away, ashamed. I went home and told my mom. She washed my clothes that night – a dark purple velveteen pantsuit. All I knew was this: waiting was simply what women and girls did while men and boys in the mirror-image door opposite breezed in and breezed out. I internalized the supposed reasons – women were doing their makeup, gabbing, taking too long. For men, the bathroom is an eyes-ahead in-and-out; for women, allegedly, it's some kind of potty party. A pee parade. But here's the thing: I've never seen a woman do more than pat down some stray hairs or slash a strip of lipstick across her mouth in a public bathroom. Without the benefit of knowing what's going on in the opposite room, men have made judgments about women, while women have been left wondering what the heck is causing all the lines.

Except Clara Greed. She's one of the women who sleuthed it out.

The story of how Clara Greed became the UK's 'Toilet Lady' finds its genesis at Paddington Station with a pay-toilet turnstile and an ill-mannered station manager. When the central London transit station was refurbished in the early 1990s, pay gates were installed at the entrance to its basement-level public toilets. The facilities had been free since 1963's Public Lavatories Act made it illegal to put pay turnstiles in front of any public convenience. The turnstile part of that statute was repealed in 1981, and then, one day, without warning, there were nasty mechanical gates staring at Clara Greed.

Something lit a fire under her that day. She passed through Paddington regularly and just as regularly used the toilets there. She was furious. But not just about the twenty-pence fee. She was furious that the toilets had been renovated but left down a steep set of steps into the basement. She was furious that the turnstiles were excluding people from freely going about their natural bodily business. She was furious that the toilets were suddenly no longer the province of anyone visiting Paddington. She was furious that public bathroom provision – which she knew intuitively was a human right, even if her work and her teaching hadn't brought her to the point of saying it outright yet – was being hacked away when it ought to have been improving. She phoned up the station manager when she got home. They fought. He ended the call with a suggestion for Greed. 'If you want to go to the toilet,' he told her, 'you can go round the hedge!'

Greed calls this her 'conversion experience.' The urban planner and rock-ribbed feminist launched an inadvertent career as a defender of free and abundant public bathroom access, focused particularly on the needs of women. 'Through no fault of my own,' she says, 'I became the Toilet Lady.' Today, Greed is an emerita professor in the Architecture and the Built Environment faculty at the University of the West of England in Bristol. 'I don't look like a dirty-minded toilet campaigner,' she jokes. But that's never stopped others from looking at her that way. Because almost invariably, Greed has found herself delivering a difficult truth to architects, planners, and municipal governments: when it comes to public bathrooms, you're really screwing up.

One of the most visible problems is, ironically, one few in those professions seem able to see – the leagues of women waiting for the can in public buildings. What that's about, Greed says, isn't the women. It's the washrooms. Try this counting trick next time you're out: even when floor space is equal for men's and women's restrooms, men often get more provision. Where women get six cubicles, men might get four cubicles plus four urinals. Consider the Pavilion toilets I spent so many days trying to get into with my kids – three toilets and two urinals on the men's side and four toilets on the women's.

But that's not where the inequality ends. Women, biologically, need more provision. For one thing, they take longer to empty their bladders. I've been rhyming off the most-cited numbers since I first started researching toilet design problems in the early aughts: men take, on average, forty-five seconds to pee; women, ninety-six. A 2017 study out of Ghent University in Belgium cites times of sixty seconds for men and ninety for women. Pretty close and point taken. But women also spend more time because they have to squeeze into a stall, close the door, lock it (if you're a man, ask a close-by woman how frequently bathroom slide locks are misaligned). Women must take down or remove clothing to urinate. Most men walk in, unzip, and let 'er rip. And third: women use the bathroom more frequently than men. Again, biology: women menstruate, women can be pregnant. But also, society: women are more likely to be care-givers for children, the elderly, and the disabled. 'The men, as you know,' Greed says, 'waltz in and out.'

Or don't. In the absence of a toilet, desperate men, by virtue of simple mechanics, can easily pee *en plein air*. This biological ace card also adds options to the provision men get inside build-ings. Men can use toilets, regular urinals, and trough urinals – pretty much any hole with a sewer-heading drain will do for an able-bodied man. Women pee in toilets; ergo, they need toilets in their bathrooms – which helps contribute to the unequal ratios in men's versus women's rooms. Urinals simply take up less room. So where square footage for men's and women's bath-rooms is equal, men usually get more opportunities to go.

Urinals are efficient and effective, no question. But urinals for women have largely been a non-starter. American Standard sold one in the 1950s, but uptake was slow, probably because of the increasing popularity of women wearing trousers. It was discontinued. Portable urine-diverting devices like the P-Mate – which we'll meet again in a later chapter – are considered by most women articles of last resort. And cisgendered women aren't the only ones left out. While some trans women might have the bodily equipment to use urinals, if they're using the women's rooms that match their gender, they won't find any urinals in there. Some trans men will not have the equipment to use urinals, even when they find them in the men's rooms they are rightly using. Short take on the universal usefulness of urinals? It's a toilet, toilet, toilet, toilet world.

Compounding the problem: men dominate planning, design, and construction. When Greed studied architecture and planning at Cardiff University in the 1980s, she was one of only four women. And all the professors were men. The male-to-female ratios in these fields aren't much better today, especially among the ranks of 'starchitects' whose splashy, celebrated art can fall shy of practicality, particularly when it comes to women's needs. Off the top of her head, Greed cites Jonathan Adams's Wales Millennium Centre in Cardiff and Paul Andreu's Dubai International Airport Terminal 3. 'Huge queues. It's atrocious. A major thing like this and they can't even provide toilets.'

Men, Greed has discovered, don't appreciate her investigations into their bathroom business. 'Talking about how many urinals should be provided or how long it takes men to urinate – some people probably think a girl shouldn't know these kinds of things.' And pee is mild on the spectrum of Greed's favourite topics. Periods, Greed says, make men go red. 'I used to be very professional and technical,' she tells me, 'and now I don't care. I just say what I want to say.'

How much money, I wonder, would you have if you tallied up all the dimes collected in automated stall-lock pay toilets in the 1970s and 1980s across North America? Pay-to-pee, for a time, wasn't unexceptional in the United States and Canada. The early twentieth century saw the burgeoning of this trend, which spider-webbed its way across the continent by way of transit terminals and shopping malls. By the 1970s, it's estimated there were fifty thousand pay toilets in the United States. Ten cents a tinkle.

Pay toilets were flushed out of America by the efforts of a small committee of free-weeing advocates known as CEPTIA – the Committee to End Pay Toilets in America, about which the journalist Aaron Gordon wrote a colourful narrative history in 2014 in *Pacific Standard* magazine. Cooked up at a Howard Johnson pay toilet off the Pennsylvania Turnpike by two brothers and proselytized by their friends and family, CEPTIA argued that elimination is inevitable – dime or no dime – and demanding money for a basic bodily function is a violation of human rights. Moreover, CEPTIA argued, stall locks represented discrimination against women, since urinals usually remained free. The feminist argument was the one that hit hardest in Equal Rights Amendment–engrossed mid-seventies America. First city – and soon state – governments banned the locks.

Locks were part of the scenery at the local mall when I was growing up in Dartmouth, Nova Scotia, a suburb of Halifax. I remember always stopping in to get a dime from my grandmother, who worked at the House of Bridal Fashions. Other times, I slithered under the stall door to avoid the charge (a dime clearly meant more to me then). Apparently, I wasn't alone: Gordon's history notes the four techniques of foiling stall locks, rolled out by CEPTIA (who, besides being a grassroots social-justice powerhouse, was also delightfully jocular) at a press conference in 1973. There was my own 'American Crawl'; the 'Doorman,' where one user holds the door for the next; the 'Stick It,' in which a piece of Scotch tape invisibly covers the lock, preventing it from engaging; and the 'Stuff' – same idea, but with toilet paper rammed into the hole.

I recall witnessing that technique at the mall. Wait. Or do I? Bob Pasquet was a manager at the shopping centre of my childhood and preteen indolence, and he remembers those diabolical dime-purloiners controlling access to the *outside* of the main bathroom door, not the individual stalls. (Then why the heck was I sliding my body along the grotty old bathroom floor – ew! – instead of just opening the door?) I canvassed the memories of childhood friends. Some sided with Pasquet, others with me. There's this, too: I remember locks in the 1980s. Pasquet says they were removed about 1977, too early for me to remember them. Here's what's certain, anyway: women shoppers lugging bedraggled children would routinely march into Pasquet's office to complain. 'I always tried to convince them that they were better off paying a dime,' Pasquet says, 'and pretty well anybody can afford a dime, and if you didn't have a dime, you could get one from pretty well any store. In my opinion, they stopped some vandalism.' But not all. Men would knock the stall doors off their hinges and smash the toilet paper holders. Women, Pasquet says, weren't as inclined to lavatory savagery, but were messier. 'Toilet paper and all sorts of awful.' He wonders if the vandalism was an ironic product of people's anger over having to pay. Still, he says, 'I don't remember a lot of controversy.'

After my chat with Pasquet, I wondered about the alleged bad manners of women. My husband worked in a bar in his twenties and had to clean the bathrooms after his shift. He once echoed Pasquet's comments, saying: 'All those tiny pieces of toilet paper all over the floor. I never understood it.' Then it struck me – all those minuscule pieces represent something much bigger. Women don't just wait in lines to use public bathrooms, we actually use bathrooms differently than men. We have more parts of the bathroom to navigate. We can't really stand up to pee, so when we're faced with a particularly dirty seat, many women choose to hover. It's an excellent quadriceps-hamstring workout, I'll grant, but it usually ends up leaving more splashed pee on the seat for the next person. Having a properly operating and adequately stocked bathroom is worth more to women, because we rely on the function and inventory more.

First: men don't use toilet paper at urinals. (Look, just admit it.) Even the ones who opt for stalls don't bother wiping when they urinate, or, at least, they don't wipe as commonly as women. There's more toilet paper mess in women's bathrooms because women actually *use* the stuff. And there's so much on the floor because of the half-assed design of commercial toilet paper dispensers, the kind of paper they hold, and the way they're installed. To start, the paper is single-ply, wraithlike; you need great gobs of the stuff to get anything done with it. It's manufactured on hulking rolls the size of extra-large pizzas, the weight of the things so heavy compared to the lightness of the toilet tissue that one semi-aggressive pull instantly rips it. The plastic dispensers are likewise no match for the beef of those giant rolls, so the paper clunks out in frustrating stop-starts. And here's the kicker: the dispensers are, so often, installed too low – women are grabbing up and under at the paper from a trapped seated position. The paper flies off in Lilliputian bits as we awkwardly tug.

And yet...how can this be?! Anyone accustomed to sitting on a public toilet and using toilet paper could ferret out the appropriate height for a dispenser. Here's my stab at the reason that simple user-friendliness is so elusive inside the toilet cubicle: men install the dispensers. It hearkens back to the point Clara Greed made to me when she was laying out the reasons women so often wait in bathroom lines: men dominate planning, design, and construction. Men aren't the ones usually sitting on public toilets to pee, scrounging for paper to wipe. Women are. But women either aren't doing the installing, or they aren't being asked what works and why.

So, as women sit on the toilet clawing at the paper; as we work with more complex clothing, and live the biological fact of taking longer to empty our bladders than men; as we change tampons and children's diapers and assist elderly relatives – what happens? Lines form for women's bathrooms. Longer and longer and longer. I mean, just ask Hillary Clinton. In December 2015, the then presidential hopeful was late getting back to the stage after a commercial break during a live televised Democratic debate. As the moderator posed a question to Bernie Sanders about median household income, Clinton strode to her podium, in front of the cameras, her opponents, and 6.7 million viewers and pronounced a deadpan 'Sorry.' Turns out, she was in a lineup for the ladies' room. The solution here, and for every woman kept waiting in line, isn't to fix the women. Women aren't what's broken. What's broken is bathrooms. And the fix is potty parity.

Potty parity is a movement that seeks to reduce bathroom waiting time for women by treating men and women, boys and girls, equally. Which is to say, unequally – because, as we've seen, an equal number of toilets does not make for equal waiting time. So the 'parity' ratios mean an increase for women: sometimes there are two facilities for females to every one facility for males; sometimes it's 3:1; sometimes it's 3:2. Potty parity begs the question: Why should women have to wait and men not have to? Ask yourself, and you'll find there's no good reason – it's garden-variety gender discrimination. That's why the American Restroom Association has been fighting the parity battle since the 1990s and has seen legislation passed at the municipal and state levels. New York City, Philadelphia, California, Minnesota, Pennsylvania, Tennessee, Texas, Washington, and other jurisdictions have all enacted parity laws recognizing the greater needs of women.

Canada has potty parity laws, too. The National Building Code of Canada enshrines 2:1 provision in favour of women, and most Canadian provinces and territories have adopted the rules wholesale. Yet, if you're keeping track, the Halifax Common Pavilion bathrooms I've been telling you about rank 5:4 in favour of men. What's up with that? you ask. What's up is the intractability of many public bathroom problems – laws apply only to new construction, and older bathrooms aren't subject to parity code until they're extensively renovated. We may be starting to think about equity, at least from a statutory level, but we're still using the same damn bathrooms.

The fight for potty parity goes beyond the battle for more stalls. It's about getting more bathroom access generally in cities, because women need bathrooms more often than men. Mandating governments to provide public bathrooms at all, let alone to build up standards for the numbers of public bathrooms that should exist based on population, has mostly eluded public toilet advocates. Bathrooms are a political football; their existence is often by the grace of business improvement organizations or parks associations, rather than by law.

While potty parity is squarely about women and people who identify as female – we've all got the same problem if we're in the lineup under the stick figure wearing the skirt – more and better bathrooms don't benefit women alone. People with invisible disabilities like incontinence, shy bladder syndrome, and inflammatory bowel disease all get a lift from more loos. So do parents of small children and caregivers of adults. There are scores of bathroom users out there who could really use the leg up.

Clara Greed knows that her favoured bathroom fixes – including double provision for women and wider stalls – are hard to swallow for governments and businesses. They stretch budgets as they reach for parity. She often hears how challenging retrofits that make more space for women can be. 'There won't be any room left for a stage,' one theatre-owner whined to her. 'It's going to all be women's toilets.' Governments, at least those up the food chain with the job of legislating changes rather than paying for them, have been more receptive. Greed herself helped write the UK government's standard on public toilet provision.

The planner is at home with the stodginess of committees and code by way of her training. But she's unrepentantly grounded in the practical. No wonder. Greed is a woman. She waits in bathroom lines just like the rest of us. Or, perhaps, *un*like the rest of us, who fail to notice the injustice or who pass it off as the way things are. 'I do toilet evangelism standing there in the queue,' she says. 'You need to raise consciousness.' Greed wants to lead a revolution, and not the velvet sort.

If there's any revolution happening in public bathrooms now, though, it's being driven by the transgender community. Trans individuals often report feeling out of place in public bathrooms, which are typically strictly sex-segregated and tightly policed by users. To wit: most people, I'd wager, would walk silently past someone they suspected was shooting drugs in a stall. Yet watch a man step foot into the women's bathroom and he'll be urgently ushered out for his social transgression. My dad once accidentally strolled into the women's room at a ski hill as my young daughter tried frantically to alert him. We still talk and laugh about it years later.

This is not the experience of trans people using public bathrooms that fit their gender. Being transgender in a gendered bathroom is rarely funny. Trans people report facing verbal and physical threats and abuse in the bathrooms that are right for their gender, but can be perceived by others as not matching their sex. A solution is unisex or gender-neutral or gender-free (my preferred term) bathrooms, which are being embraced in public schools and universities across North America, in chain restaurants like Tim Hortons, and in government buildings. In 2013, then Philadelphia mayor Michael Nutter signed legislation requiring such bathrooms in city-owned buildings; it's the same in Oregon's Multnomah County, which includes Portland. But on several fronts, gender-liberated bathrooms fail.

The legislation mostly works like potty parity – only for new construction, so it can take a long time for change to happen. When it does, not everyone's on board. The conversion from traditional side-by-side, sex-separated bathrooms with multiple stalls to single-user bathrooms may level the peeing field, but it is wickedly expensive and usually decreases provision and adds to lineups. Where once there may have been two stalls in the women's and a stall and three urinals for men – allowing six people to go at once (unfairly benefiting men, I grant) – there may now be two toilets in two single-occupant rooms that are designated gender-free or 'family.' In the less commonly seen conversion to gender neutrality – where signs are simply replaced to declare multi-stall spaces gender-free – there's been backlash ranging from outright transphobic to merely wary. Even declaring existing single stalls gender-free has its detractors.

Clara Greed, for her part, likes the idea of gender-free washrooms, but won't stand for them if it means the removal of women-only spaces. She points out the prohibition against sharing such space with biological males among some Muslim women, fundamentalist Christian women, Hindu women, and Orthodox Jewish women. She says there's a social function of public bathrooms that's being lost with sex desegregation: 'The public toilet is one of the few places left where women can be actually separated from men.'

Uprisings of any stripe are becoming more complicated, at least in England and its surrounds. Whereas North Americans, and certainly Canadians, haven't enjoyed much on-street public provision, the UK has a long tradition of recognizing the need for stand-alone public bathrooms in city centres (even if they have been designed, in the main, for men – more on that in chapter six). But today, public toilets are disappearing. A 2016 BBC report found, through Freedom of Information requests, that at least 1,782 facilities had closed across the UK in the preceding decade. In London alone, it's estimated that about half of council-managed public bathrooms have closed: city governments don't see their value justifying the cost of their maintenance. Some of London's ornate underground Victorian-era facilities are being sold off and transformed into kicky little cafés and hip restaurants. I love charcuterie, sure, but there is a limit. Today's toilet campaigns, increasingly, aren't for better provision, but to keep what's there now.

Greed turns to the business case. When visitors come to Britain, she says, 'they are disgusted by our public toilets and the lack of facilities.' But she's also convinced that better provision helps breathe life into dusty downtowns. Public bathrooms, she argues, are far from money down the drain. 'I keep asking god for a toilet miracle, but I haven't seen one yet. It's like the miracle of the five thousand loaves and fishes. I want five thousand more toilets.'

3

SOME HISTORICAL SHIT

Someone wipes her bottom, drops a pre-moistened flushable wipe into the toilet bowl, and watches the swirling mess sloosh south. In a restaurant down the street, an employee pours the dregs of a kettle of fryer oil into a sink drain and watches the warm, lardish goo gurgle down. Then each walks away from the place her home or work connects to the underground wonder of the modern sewer. I mean, that's how it's supposed to go, right? The sewers lie waiting for our worst. They accept our shit, our shower water, and our tampons; our flushable wipes, used medications, and the leftover fat from our Sunday-morning bacon and eggs. Our approach to sewers is dump and run. We rarely give these accepting labyrinthine marvels a thought.

Until the sewers push back.

The pipe leading from that home and the pipe exiting that restaurant connect at a trunk line, well below the sidewalk and street. By this point, the hot fat is no longer hot. And the flushable wipe, while flushable in name, is not in nature – wipes are designed to withstand being wet for long periods in storage and hold their shape even in the face of sustained abuse. The wipe enters the trunk line as durable as ever, swimming along with dozens of equally sturdy tampons, applicators, and used condoms.

It snags on a sewer wall. On it, the congealing fryer fat finds a home. More fat from more restaurants passes and sticks. More wipes from more homes greet the tumescent mess, along with more tampons, more sanitary pads… You get the scene. The New York City Department of Environmental Protection estimated in 2015 that wet wipes had cost the city $18 million for blockage-clearing and disposal over the previous five years. And used cooking oil is a problem for sewers all over. Austin, Texas; Washington, D.C.; and Tulsa, Oklahoma, have all started ad campaigns begging homeowners to quit dumping leftovers down their sinks. Animal fats, vegetable oils, and lard – even dairy products – stick to the walls of sewers like cholesterol plaque on the inside of an artery.

The frightening apotheosis of this problem is the mythically dubbed fatberg – a terrifying blob that adheres to the walls of sewers like concrete. A fatberg the size of a double-decker bus was discovered under Kingston in 2013 by Thames Water, London, England's water and sewage utility. In 2017, the biggest fatberg on record was discovered under the Whitechapel district, the kind of monster that makes the 2013 Kingston fatberg sound quaint: more than ten times bigger, and longer than two football pitches. The Museum of London put a portion of it on display in 2018 (exhibition title: *Fatberg!*). Thames Water crews – eight members strong, working seven days a week – took two and a half months to remove this puppy. No doubt all the while looking over their shoulders for the next fatberg around the sewer bend.

See, these things really do pop up out of nowhere. Sure, it seems wild to imagine something growing, undetected, underneath your house that's the length of eleven double-decker buses, like the Whitechapel fatberg. But the whopping great volumes of oil from restaurant fryers and residential cooking, congealing around sewer joints and the reams of wet wipes, collect bit by bit by tiny bit. One frying pan of bacon fat? How could that hurt? A tampon here? Some dental floss there? No biggie. No one pictures these minor cast-offs mixing with gelling blubber to become a sturdy fecal-fat blob looming below the asphalt. Yet Thames Water clears some forty thousand fat blockages a year. The pinguid terror of the Kingston fatberg was only discovered when residents reported trouble getting their toilets to flush. As Simon Evans, a Thames Water spokesman, told the *Guardian*, technicians discovered a 'heaving, sick-smelling, rotting mass of filth and feces' stuck to the roof of a neighbourhood trunk line. The good news? Kingston upon Thames avoided – narrowly – having the contents of its every toilet bubbling up out of powder-room loos and laundry-room sinks.

Modern city sewer systems, despite the abuse they withstand, have limits. And in growing cities, it's not only flushing the unflushable and draining the undrainable that sinks the sewers, it's a simple question of volume: the more of us there are, the more shit we collectively produce. And the more shit we produce, the better we have to be at finding different ways of dealing with it. Humans have the benefit of millennia in our back pockets on this one. But *different* and *better* aren't exactly the hallmarks of our relationship with removing what we excrete. Consider: North Americans and Europeans sit down daily to poo into water we've spent gobs of cash to purify to drinking quality. It's, well…stupid. Why treat water only to foul it with bacteria- and microbe-laden turds and flush it away? Because we started doing it that way a long time ago, built massive unretrofitable plumbing and sewage systems to support our little quirk, and haven't found the will or the way to shake it since.

We're married to our toilets. But we're sticking together more out of habit than love. And perhaps out of fear of what we'd do without them. Toilets long before the toilet we know today were mere ditches in the ground. In Deuteronomy 23:12–14, Moses lays out a biblical code for where and how to relieve thyself, and the Bible, on this count, is the quintessence of right-headedness: walk away from areas where people congregate, and bring a spade to cover up your turds. (Linguistically, I'll grant, the scripture is more elegant.) Moses was a sensible fellow, clearly, but I suspect he was codifying custom rather than making headline news. In ancient cities, things got more complicated. It's harder to get away from your neighbours when there are forty thousand of them, as there were in Jesus-era Jerusalem. Soon enough, many great civilizations – Indians, Chinese, Babylonians, and Minoans among them – figured out that water worked brilliantly to wash away waste. But no one rocked early sewage removal like the Ancient Romans. They employed aqueducts to move water, reused grey water from their public baths for irrigation, and, like many other cultures, collected urine and feces as fertilizers for growing food. The Roman sewer system during the time of Pliny the Elder served a whopping one million urban dwellers altogether.

And all together.

In the Roman Empire, toilets were public. And public meant really, *really* public – a dozen or more citizens sitting together shooting the shit. You can shelve your horror. The idea of toilet privacy as we know it today is something no ancient ever experienced. Historians believe there may have been screens or other means of separating the users of these mostly outdoor latrines, but using public facilities was a decidedly communal event. These toilets were located at central, easy-to-access spots, like the backs of theatres and near markets. They comprised long benches with holes over running water to draw away waste. Another spring-water channel in front of users' feet was used for cleaning. It seems Romans dipped a sponge on a stick into the water and used the moistened swab to scrub their derrières. All this, in the presence of, sometimes, twenty-five or more fellow citizens. Roman-style communal latrines dotted Hadrian's Wall in the north and extended south through the empire. Not-so-private public privies were hot in Roman times perhaps not only because people enjoyed the company of their neighbours, but because the disposal of waste was, itself, a public interest. The Romans engaged in building all sorts of community infrastructure – it is the empire's claim to fame. So, their embrace of latrines was a product of enlightenment, not accident. When the empire crumbled around the fifth century, so did its toilets. And that's when the shitstorm started.

The keepers of the English language at Oxford can't say for certain where the term *loo*, a common British slang for bathroom, comes from. Though it's historically and etymologically suspect, the explanation I like best argues that *loo* comes from the French phrase '*Regardez l'eau!*' – bastardized by the English as '*Gardy loo!*' – which could accurately be translated as 'Heads up, whoever's traipsing down the street below this open window, because it's about to start raining the contents of a full chamber pot.'

There was shit, frankly, sloshed all over medieval Europe. It was tossed from homes into street-level ditches. It was launched from holes in settlement walls. It rotted in turgid cesspits. It bunged up rivers that once freely flowed. The sewer sense of the Roman Empire may not have been perfect – they too allowed waste into rivers and steams – but their successors literally threw their advances out the window. London's first major sanitary acts weren't passed until the thirteenth century. They prohibited pigs from running (and, presumably, shitting) in the streets, and demanded an end to on-street tallow-rendering, solder-melting, and the flaying of dead horses. By 1300, people were asked to please stop hurling their poo into the streets. All solid ideas, for sure. Except no one seemed to do much about them. Animals and humans and all their sundry waste communed endlessly in cities and villages.

There was little in the way of organized sewage disposal. The population of High Middle Ages Europe was about eighty million; in overcrowded urban spaces, bodies were everywhere and so were their by-products. Writer Bill Bryson notes in his book *At Home: A Short History of Private Life* that Italian adventurer Giacomo Casanova, on a visit to London, frequently 'saw someone "ease his sluices" in full public view along roadsides or against buildings.'

Science writer David Waltner-Toews, in *The Origin of Feces: What Excrement Tells Us about Evolution, Ecology, and a Sustainable Society*, calls the narrative of shit 'one of fits and starts.' It's an apt characterization. The oldest recorded 'flush' toilet was at Crete's palace of Knossos, dating from 1700 BCE. That might as well have been a ghost loo; it mysteriously disappeared. The Romans got things chugging along nicely, then screwed the sanitation pooch when they lost the empire. Exceptions also punctuated the medieval era of dire squalidity – Henry III ordered the maintenance of a Thames-bound underground drainage system at Palace of Westminster and watercourses ran under some monastery dormitories. Tudor times saw the establishment of drop toilets – seats with open bottoms that either hung over exterior castle moats or were built inside closets in homes (and from which feces and urine dropped down into a basement cesspit). The idea was for the poo to fall away from the poo-ers. Pity the wretched workers who had to hand-clean the moats and dig out the basement trenches, not least of all because excavations of medieval and Tudor privies suggest humans were bursting with parasites. The job of the so-called night-soil man wasn't an envied one. Sir John Harington, the godson of Queen Elizabeth I, built the first mechanical flush toilet in 1596, installing one at Richmond Palace for Her Majesty and one in his own home. The Queen mustn't have been all that amused. She died seven years later, and the Harington model was never seen again.

Outhouses and chamber pots proved fecally sufficient for the next two centuries, until an explosion of lavatorial concoctions based on Harington's original flusher hit England in the last quarter of the eighteenth century. First came Alexander Cummings, an horologist; next, Joseph Bramah, a locksmith; after them, loads more inventors got into the game. You'll want to know here about the name synonymous with early water closets: Thomas Crapper. Let me flush your assumptions. Crapper did not invent the toilet, and the slang word *crap* predates the man himself. He was a plumber by trade, and a genius marketer by nature. Crapper created the first bathroom showroom, distributing the inventions of others and adding his company name to the fixtures. He was a whiz at nudging forward the desirability of indoor outhouses. Though as the Victorian era progressed, our collective Western disgust at urine and feces began to fix and intensify and our relationship with getting rid of our waste changed indelibly.

Conjure the stench of two and a half million bowel-loads of feces dropped daily into the Thames. Imagine it combined with the ascending Hades of a London summer. Imagine all that feces and urine, plus whatever else – animal corpses, rotten food, industrial waste – Londoners felt like chucking into the Thames, literally fermenting in the June heat. Picture the top of the city's main river as a bubbly fecal froth. No surprise they dubbed the summer of 1858 the Great Stink.

Now picture Joseph Bazalgette to the rescue, a hero in mutton-chops. Bazalgette was the civil engineer who designed London's modern sewage system. He was first put to the task during the Great Stink, when olfactory offensiveness reached such heights that the curtains of Parliament were closed and doused with lime chloride, and London's flâneurs held perfumed cloths to their noses and mouths, lest they faint from the fetor. It was gross.

It's not as if everything had been hunky-dorky in London before 1858. The poor suffered in close quarters with their own waste and that of their neighbours. Cesspits were the norm. The Thames and other rivers stagnated under the burden of feces (all those progressive thirteenth-century acts to help clean up the streets instructed Londoners to remove their filth and flayed horses directly to the Thames). But the Great Stink was different. It was the first time the practice of dumping raw sewage into a body of water had affected such great numbers of Londoners. Not only that, but it was the first episode, really, where it affected people who otherwise weren't much involved in taking close care of their excreta. The castle- and manor-dwelling drop-toilet crowd certainly weren't down in the moats and cesspits slopping their shit into buckets. Parliamentary caucuses weren't likely in the habit of hearing from night-soil men.

The Great Stink was just the kick in the arse needed to get the city driving toward the modern waste-management era. There was something in the air – literally, in London, but metaphorically in many other major cities, too. Paris, New York, and Toronto embarked on their modern storm and sanitary sewer systems around the same time as Bazalgette got his assignment in London. Chicago started in the 1860s; Washington, DC, in the 1880s. Many Commonwealth countries and those under colonial rule took a nod from the practices of the English and got moving on major sewer projects before the turn of the twentieth century.

That modern sewers were needed had everything to do with the rise of flush toilets from about 1800 onward. Toilets after early tinkerers Cummings and Bramah were increasingly reliable and less smelly – and so more welcome inside homes. Barbara Penner, the architectural historian, has found evidence of about two hundred thousand dotting London around the time of the Great Stink, adding volume to the Thames' woes Bazalgette was charged with making better. It could have been worse – indoor flush toilets at this time were firmly the preserve of England's wealthy, a norm that lasted into the 1920s. Multi-family outhouses were common in some urban areas even through the 1960s and 1970s. If the Great Stink almost shut down Parliament, imagine how much greater the stink if flush toilets had then been as common as they are today.

What the indoor bathroom also changed was the notion that toileting (and, for that matter, bathing) was a communal exercise. With interior water closets, it became possible to enjoy complete privacy while urinating and defecating. And with the flush mechanism, it became possible to instantly flush away one's own feces and urine. To plausibly pretend that bodies did not excrete. After all, even drop-toilet users could see and smell those piles of fecal mush below them.

Over time, the luxury of privacy morphed into a must-have. It became not only desirable to be alone on the can, but necessary for anyone who wanted to stay on the right side of morality. People who did not practise solo toileting were regarded as lacking in decency. And that went double for women. An inescapable physical function became shameful. It's difficult to overstate the impact this prudery had on Western culture. It's front and centre today in our toilet humour, and in the epic number of euphemisms we employ to talk about excreting. A notion grew along with the status-symbol toilet: sharing a bathroom with those outside your family was something to avoid. It's even come to the point, today, that we don't want to smell, hear, or feel any evidence, such as warm toilet seats, of those who've gone before us. Bathrooms remain one of our central taboos. So, by early in Queen Victoria's reign, private pooing had become a mark of prestige. The masses, of course, wanted it. And George Jennings would give it to them.

Jennings, a sanitary engineer, installed the first public flushing toilets in London – for both men and women – at the Great Exhibition of 1851. Jennings installed his 'monkey closets' at the Crystal Palace, the almost one-million-square-foot temporary building set up in Hyde Park from May through October to house the exhibition. These inaugural public conveniences boasted lush waiting rooms and two dozen attendants. Users paid a penny or halfpenny for access to small private cupboards with flush toilets inside. The monkey closets were a marker of national pride and a banner of English technological progress to show off to the twenty-eight countries represented at the fair. Historian Lucinda Lambton notes in her book *Temples of Convenience & Chambers of Delight* that women in the nineteenth century suffered embarrassment at the idea of water closets. No doubt – they lived in a society that told them to act that way. (A history of Thomas Crapper & Co. says women were given to fainting at the mere sight of his window displays.) But some, at least, overcame their shame. Jennings's closets were used more than eight hundred thousand times over the course of the exhibition. The Crystal Palace toilets were a watershed. They gave many Londoners their first look at (and first chance to try) flush toilets. They also gave regular citizens the idea that flush toilets and urinals could – and perhaps *should* – be a matter of public concern.

Public bathrooms increasingly became conveniences of moral, political, and hygienic necessity – not to mention sparkling exemplars of nation-building. Little expense was spared in building them in the UK's major centres. Public toilets in England's largest cities became a proud part of the urban landscape (though many were actually underground, often in response to surrounding business owners who linked public bathrooms with impropriety). Their entrances were magnificent, their urinals and countertops marble, their windows leaded stained glass, and their fixtures ornate. Dignitaries dedicated them. Americans and Canadians swelled with the same pride – and no dearth of competitiveness – in providing public health benefits to city dwellers. In the second half of the nineteenth century, free public baths and pools were built in major US cities. Toronto constructed lavish underground on-street public conveniences with attendants and services like shoe shining and boot cleaning.

Jennings's Crystal Palace monkey closets were what pushed toilets into the spotlight, allowing them to transform in the public imagination from private luxury to urban necessity. And seven years later, London's Great Stink was the movement that turned the bowels of the city's jury-rigged sewer system into a public project and a civic responsibility.

But it wasn't all guts and glory.

As the twentieth century progressed, on-street bathrooms mushroomed in the UK, and their installation became common in the US and Canada in transit stations, shopping centres, airports, and other commercial and public buildings. Built into all of them were design and access barriers, and built into those impediments was a series of fights about the right to public space that would continue through that century and beyond. Despite the public-good zeitgeist that surrounded them, early-twentieth-century Western public bathrooms cemented themselves as places for able, adult, white men. And not many others.

Crystal Palace aside, women were largely left out of this provision parade. In fact, it wasn't until four decades after the Great Exhibition, in 1893, that the first permanent public toilets for women were installed on London's Strand. In Toronto, early on-street public bathrooms were, likewise, built only for men. Even in locations where women later enjoyed conveniences alongside men's, the number of water closets for them were dwarfed by the number for men, who also had urinals. Women's public conveniences were diabolically chicken-and-eggish at this time. The dearth of toilets both reflected that women weren't out of the house as much as men and reinforced that women *could* not go out, lest they be caught short due to the lack of provision. In any case, very few working-class women were able to afford the common penny or halfpenny fee. (Men were only required to pay for the use of water closets; public urinals were free.)

In reality, women had begun to travel urban areas in great numbers as part of the growing workforce many years before, during the Industrial Revolution – but they weren't always visible. A certain level of denial was at play here, on the part of men and women who couldn't handle the upheaval to women's 'natural' place in the home – quite simply, people refused to acknowledge that women were part of city life. There were also myriad measures in place that hid women in plain sight. For example, the main branch of the Bank of Nova Scotia in Halifax was built in 1931 with a separate 'ladies' banking room.' (Today, I understand, it's someone's office, so though I am a lady – ha! – I was allowed to pay the balance of my car loan at a regular teller.) Early children's public bathroom needs were even more unspoken than women's, so family bathrooms and changing tables were unthinkable. Forget 'seen and not heard' – when it came to public toilet provision for children in the nineteenth century, it was more like *not* seen and not heard.

It's not surprising that the first of the great post-Victorian public bathroom campaigns argued that women needed provision that at least mirrored men's. But women and children weren't the only ones being left out of the potty party. Aids for people with mobility challenges started to creep into private homes and institutions mid-twentieth-century, but few, if any, grab bars, deep sinks, or larger stalls were found in public bathrooms. In the US, standards for accessibility were laid out in 1961. The rules were the world's first, which deserves some ballyhooing, but they lacked any accompanying legal stipulations. It wasn't until the 1990s that accessibility regulations were actually enforced throughout the US, the UK, and Canada. Up to that point, wheelchair users took a chance when they left their houses; they could find themselves in any public building or on any downtown street without a bathroom to use. And as we'll see, the fight is far from over.

The challenging of racially segregated public bathrooms wasn't quite so slow-moving, but what it lacked in red tape, it made up in blood. A bathroom-by-bathroom, drinking-fountain-by-drinking-fountain movement took place across the US starting in 1961, when groups of self-organized Freedom Riders travelled by plane, train, and bus through the American South. Along their travels, they undertook the deceptively simple acts of loitering in waiting areas or using public facilities – white Freedom Riders used 'Coloreds Only' public spaces and African-American Freedom Riders used facilities labelled as separate for whites. Their actions were to ensure that the December 1960 Supreme Court ruling forbidding discrimination in transportation services against interstate passengers was being upheld.

It wasn't.

Many Freedom Riders were beaten and aggressively arrested. In rural Alabama, a mob attacked a Greyhound bus carrying Freedom Riders and others. The gang of men firebombed the bus and tried to barricade the door. They then beat passengers as they escaped. Throughout the 1960s, the patchwork of Jim Crow laws that kept segregation in place legally, and allowed it to flourish socially, was dismantled. But segregation dies hard. Black and Hispanic Americans still report being denied access to public bathrooms. It's rarely overt racism these days. But the actions of store employees, who can choose who gets to use locked bathrooms and who doesn't, can amount to the same thing.

What all this toilet strife points to is how culturally constipated we are when it comes to our conception of the bathroom, and how much public bathrooms represent the ways we see others. And, of course, how resistant we humans are to change.

Bathroom fixtures went public in a big way right at the heyday of mechanized manufacturing. And when I say *fixtures*, I mean exactly that. Prefabrication became the norm for toilets, urinals, sinks, and cubicles at the end of the nineteenth century. Suddenly, bathroom components simply *were*. If users found they didn't quite fit into bathrooms, it was the users who adapted, not the hardware. It wasn't only that design variations weren't much talked about or seen. The source material the industry worked from to create designs for everyday users was drawn from a small pool of data – in the US, from studies of military personnel – and little else. (It's pretty laughable to imagine the physical measurements of young, fit military men being used to design a bathroom for my grandmother.)

Then along came Alexander Kira.

The Cornell University professor led a study from 1958 to 1965 to delve into how people actually used the bathroom. From faucets to farts, showers to the squat position, Kira wanted to scrap bathrooms – private and public – and rebuild them completely from the user's perspective. He set himself no easy task – how does one change something no one's willing to talk about? 'While we can create new technologies to satisfy our demands,' Kira wrote, 'we can also ignore particular technologies and allow them to lie idle for years.' He makes a good point: the toilet hasn't changed its essential design since George Washington was commissioned as commander-in-chief of the Continental Army.

Kira published his monumental study in book form. *The Bath-room* came out in 1966 (not to be confused with Barbara Penner's *Bathroom*). In it, he didn't just rejig existing design. He considered the psychology of bathroom use, took into account the young and the old, and didn't assume men and women approached or used bathrooms in the same ways. He conducted research in a thousand US homes and in his lab at Cornell. Kira observed, measured, and photographed men and women performing bath-room activities. *The Bathroom* was a quantitative and qualitative jackpot. It concerned itself, for example, not only with the ideal dimensions for a bathtub in order for a woman to fit into it, but with how the bathtub could be sized and shaped to accommodate the different positions she might use for relaxing, to clean herself, and to enter and exit the bath.

Kira didn't picture one bathroom for the young or able and a completely different one for the old or infirm. He saw the ideal bathroom as a versatile space – with uniform safety measures for any users who needed them because of age or temporary or permanent disability. He saw the bathroom as a space that should be easy to modify for changing bodies and changing needs – a bathroom for a lifetime.

The Bathroom is fascinating because of the way Kira both listened to what his subjects told him and, frankly, didn't. On one hand, he suggested bathroom changes based on what study participants reported would work better, respecting their intu-ition. He wanted higher sinks that didn't require hunching over for adults to use. He wanted them shamrock-shaped, so that the water would spread instead of splash, and with faucets that would spray in an arc for drinking. But he also came up with stuff that the people he studied likely never would have come up with, or which they probably would have laughed at. One of his sugges-tions was a conventional toilet with added foot pegs for modified squatting – picture little foot holders near the top of the bowl, toward the back; using them would situate your knees a little above belly-button-level as you sat on the toilet. Squat defecation is uncommon in the West, and it's unlikely to have been the position any of Kira's mostly middle-class US research subjects would have settled into to have a poo. But Kira's research, and others' since, shows that squatting both makes it easier to fully clear the bowels and decreases the likelihood of hemorrhoids, among other medical conditions. Kira pushed for modified squatting, even though it went against the cultural norm.

Why don't we all squat to shit, anyway, if it's so much better for us? In a word: culture. Just as we've had a hard time, historically, changing our understanding of who deserves space in public bathrooms and what it means to guarantee different user groups a seat, we also resist design changes. An example is the bidet, which more effectively cleans the perineal area than toilet paper (assuming people wash their hands well after using it; otherwise the hygiene benefit is wiped out). The bidet has never taken off in North America, even though we pride ourselves on over-the-top cleanliness. Japan-based toilet manufacturer Toto has been making the Toto Washlet, a combo toilet-bidet with a heated seat and oscillating spout, since the 1980s: Toto's net sales in the 2016–17 fiscal were US$311 million. But less than 25 percent came from outside Japan. We in the West prefer, instead, to ineffectually scrape at the remnants of our last bowel movements with dry, rip-prone toilet paper. We use soap and water to clean every other part of our bodies, but not the dirtiest. (The market for flushable wipes *has* more than tripled in the past decade, but it's at best a halfway measure, and one causing full-blown, fatbergian grief to urban sewer systems.)

For our bodies to meet the bathroom in different ways requires, perhaps, that our brains meet the bathroom in different ways first. While *The Bathroom* is something of a bible among those who study the cultural impact and meaning of toilets, Kira's infinitely sensible modifications never really caught on with the masses. They were too far from what people were used to, and dealt with functions too far beyond the pale of bridge-game chitchat. We have preferred to let our bathroom technologies, in Kira's words, 'lie idle.'

The effects of standardization hit hardest when automation comes into play. Automated public toilets, or APTS, which dot many high-population centres, are the extreme example of a technological 'fix' to bathrooms. They were first installed in Paris in 1980, and later in the UK, the US, and around the world. In most models, users insert a coin or two to open the bathroom's door. Once it shuts, a timer starts, at the end of which the door unlocks if the user isn't already out. The timer means no one can stay in for too long. I was told by a San Francisco outreach worker that a homeless family in that city had tampered with the timer mechanism and taken up residence in one for several months, but in most APTS, the door opens in ten to fifteen minutes – long enough to use the washroom, but not enough time for a half-decent nap or any other, um, leisure activity. Once the door closes again, the devices have a wash cycle wherein the whole interior becomes like the inside of a dishwasher, sprayed and soaped and rinsed top to bottom once a user leaves (or, let's hope once she leaves – horror stories abound about users being trapped in these self-cleaning toilets, but most of the reports I've read are about children who go in alone and can't unlock the door; the fatalities are myth).

Less drastic automation has invaded everyday public bathrooms, too. Automated electric air dryers control the length of time people get to dry their hands – often too short and then, with another push of the button, too long. The motion-activated versions demand vigorous hand flapping to achieve the necessary drying time. The volume of air cannot be controlled, nor the temperature, though simple discount-store hair dryers have achieved this level of complexity. Soap comes pre-portioned, regardless of whether we need to lather our hands or faces, or clean an explosion of ketchup off a silk blouse. Water flows from taps at a predetermined volume, for a predetermined time, and at a predetermined temperature. Paper-towel dispensers decide the size of sheets we will need. Automated flushers are triggered by light, time, and movement. Irus Braverman writes incisively about all this automation hoo-ha in her essay 'Potty Training: Nonhuman Inspection in Public Washrooms' in the collection *Toilet: Public Restrooms and the Politics of Sharing*. As Braverman describes it, automated flushers assume 'a standard person with more or less standard needs engaged in an anticipated standard behavior. So it is a single individual (not with a helper or child, for example) making a single bowel movement (rather than a series) or making typical movements in a stall (not preparing for an injection, for example).' I personally defy readers – especially women – to tell me they have never been the victim of an automated flusher. So an occasional sopping backside is the price we must pay for automation? But wait, what's the benefit on our end? Better bathrooms, or so the argument goes, are less subject to some users' anti-social behaviour, such as clogging and over-filling sinks or not flushing toilets. But aren't these primarily benefits to the operators? Not the users?

Automated fixtures in public bathrooms may deter human users from messing around, but they are so narrowly controlling, they also deter activities well inside the spectrum of normal bathroom use. I'd like to be able to drink water from bathroom faucets, but what comes out is too cold for tea and too warm for refreshment, and I, lowly user that I am, cannot be trusted to decide the temperature. Even the boon to operators – that automated bathroom fixtures lessen the need for human oversight – isn't an absolute given. When automated flushers and faucets and hand dryers stop working, no human is there to know except the users, who have, precisely as a result of automation, been alienated from the space and feel no need to go out of their way to report, for example, a non-flushing and rapidly filling clogged toilet.

If there's a common theme to this book, it's this: public bathrooms are hard to get right. And no wonder. They are mired in cultural baggage, stuck in the fixedness of fixtures, and bound by massive, often ancient infrastructure. That chest-puffing Victorian desire to provide for the public was long ago flushed away. Governments today see bathrooms as more burden than duty. As I've said, in Canada, the US, and the UK, there are no statutory requirements on the part of governments to provide bathrooms to the public. So, where users dare to be too needy, and where inclusive design is hard to achieve, the government solution isn't to adapt, but to pull the plug.

This is real. Remember, half of public toilets in London, once a paragon of lavatory provision, have closed. The reasons, laid out in a 2006 Health and Public Services Committee investigation into the loss of public loos, echo with the news stories I read every day about disappearing toilets in cities all over: underground toilets, built by well-meaning but decorum-obsessed Victorians eager to provide-but-hide, are too costly to retrofit for statutory wheelchair access. Authorities are similarly cranky when it comes to non-bathroom bathroom behaviour – illicit drinking, taking drugs, or having sex (and don't forget smoking in the boys' – or girls' – room). But instead of working to curb these activities, by employing bathroom attendants, for example, governments shut them down. It's cheaper and easier to eliminate a bathroom than to work out its issues, and that's no big deal where governments have no legal responsibility to provide.

But biology's a killer. People still have to go. Media companies are leaping into the vacuum, providing on-street automated toilets that act as billions-generating billboards. Some businesses provide for immense numbers of users, banking on the knowledge that those who come for the free toilets may stay for the Caramel Frappuccino or the fries. A new bathroom business venture arose in 2014 out of the Airbnb model of people renting out temporary lodging. Airpnp was an app-based service for people seeking bathrooms in a hurry. Private toilet providers – many merely people selling access to their home bathrooms – listed their toilet and the fee for its use (anywhere from three dollars to fifteen dollars for a specified time). Airpnp, which went kaput sometime in 2016, was a far cry from the Victorian allegiance to the public good. Those early stabs at public toilets may have been wilfully ignorant of diverse needs, but at least they were spurred by concern for well-being, not money-making.

We will always produce urine and feces, and we will always, as a society, be forced to find ways to deal with it. Joseph Bazalgette's original sewer was a city-saver. But London is edging up to a population of nine million, four times the number Bazalgette built his system to serve. About fifty times a year, the system is deluged by rainwater and overflows, spurting raw sewage into the Thames – enough each time to fill a football stadium. The solution is a so-called 'super sewer,' a twenty-five-kilometre west-to-east tunnel under London, ferrying feces and overflowing stormwater to a treatment centre. It's the first time Bazalgette's mid-nineteenth-century plans have been reworked. The super sewer should be complete by 2021 and is promising to take care of the city's sewage overflow woes for a hundred years to follow. After that? Who knows.

4

VOID WHERE PROHIBITED

When someone defecates in the open – in fields and forests, on beaches, roadsides, and along train tracks – it's a public health catastrophe. The population practising open defecation has declined on average by about 22 million every year since the turn of 2000, but the most recent stats, courtesy of the World Health Organization, show that there are still about 892 million people worldwide who, as a matter of routine, poop outside.

Feces carry all manner of viruses and bacteria. The most problematic, according to the WHO, are cholera, typhoid, and hepatitis A. Even garden-variety norovirus can inflict diarrhea, nausea, vomiting, and dehydration. The cycle is eerily simple: flies feast on fresh feces and carry away germs on their tiny, hairy feet. At the next place they land – a hand, a plate of food – they deposit the germs, which make it into the mouths or noses of unwitting and unwanting humans. Germs are also brought into homes on shoes or bare feet when people accidentally walk through roadside feces and the viruses and bacteria wind up on surfaces people touch or where they prepare food. Other times, rain washes feces into wells, lakes, or rivers, which contaminates drinking water. Poor sanitation, as we know, kills 842,000 a year – almost half of them children under five.

It makes sense, then, that people with access to good sanitation live longer, healthier, and better lives. Investments in sanitation and drainage – in handwashing stations, sewage isolation and treatment, and toilets – have an astounding impact on world health.

But that only applies when people use their toilets.

A simple latrine toilet may cost only $300 to build, but usually it's not about money, says *The Big Necessity* author Rose George, who has researched sanitation and the cultural place of toilets in Southeast Asia. 'I have met young lads in India who have shown me their three-hundred-dollar smartphones. And then I say, okay, can you show me where your toilet is? And they don't have a toilet.' It's still socially acceptable to shit in public. So that's their routine. In rural northern India, a 2015 Research Institute for Compassionate Economics survey found 40 percent of households with toilets or latrines still had at least one member who preferred open defecation. 'It's the culture,' says Jack Sim. And Sim, a Singapore-based sanitation activist, has spent his life working to shift that culture, helping the world deal better with its shit. Sim founded the World Toilet Organization (the *other* wto, he's known to joke) in 2001, to spread the gospel of fecal responsibility. Even the UK's Clara Greed, widely considered the pre-eminent academic voice on public bathroom matters, reveres him. 'If anyone knows about toilets,' she told me, 'it's not me. It's Jack Sim.'

Sim made his money in the construction industry. Now retired, he works his tail off on global sanitation projects. He also makes time to chat with bathroom-obsessed journalists in Halifax from his home in Singapore. I Skyped him one lunchtime from my desk. He was on a laptop in his living room, about to see midnight hit, and offered me as much of his time as I needed. Sim's mission is simple. He wants to make toilets fashionable. Status symbols. And this brings us back to India. That country's Swachh Bharat –. 'Clean India' – mission is tackling open defecation by aiming to install enough toilets to eradicate the practice by October 2019. The initiative has seen more than 64 million toilets introduced to cities and rural areas by the government or non-profit groups. Since Swachh Bharat launched in 2014, the number of homes with toilets has risen from about 39 percent to 79 percent. Problem is, many have never been used for excretion. 'They see it as a shrine or a chicken coop,' says Sim. So it's not always lack of access that leads to open defecation. Sometimes, it's that when you've always pooped outside, that's just the way you're used to doing it.

Sim has been appointed co-convener of a project in Andhra Pradesh state in southeast India to build toilets for six million homes by the end of 2018. But the real work isn't just finding the cash to do it. It's changing the way people view the act of going to the bathroom. Sim's plan aims to make the toilet 'the happiest room' in India. 'Happiness is a universal value and, so, with humour, we say that people are happier after they visit the toilet. So, you want to be happy, you have a toilet,' says Sim. 'We ask people, "Are you happy?"' The campaign doesn't judge people for their participation in the culture of open defecation. It's not handing out dour warnings about the very real dangers of fecal contamination of water and food. It's more nuanced – both slicker and more lighthearted – than that. It's working to change the toilet from utilitarian to aspirational. Making it something people want. Something that comes with bragging rights. Like a smartphone.

Clara Greed is a little more gloomy, or, perhaps, realistic: 'It's going to take some sort of plague for people to take toilets seriously.' Or maybe a celebrity? Easing what may be the world's most pressing public health issue has gotten a boost from the Bill & Melinda Gates Foundation, which, in 2011, launched the Reinvent the Toilet Challenge, awarding grants to researchers developing new, sustainable means for dealing with human waste.

Actor Matt Damon has jumped into the global sanitation game, too, with his Water.org charity, founded with entrepreneur Gary White. The group loans money through micro-financing to people looking to improve their family's or community's sanitation and water access. It also pilots large-scale initiatives to improve sanitation. When Matt Damon talks shit, people listen.

No matter who's talking about open defecation, the safe management of human waste provides net economic benefit. The WHO estimates that every dollar invested in water and sanitation promises a $4.30 return through lowered health care costs. Thing is, that doesn't only apply to household toilets. And it doesn't only apply in the developing world. The United Nations Department of Economic and Social Affairs sees sanitation conditions as so important it uses them as a measurement tool for the overall health of a society – a core indicator of the state of human development. And if that's the case, I wonder what the UN would have to say about San Francisco.

Rachel Gordon has this perfect, awful story.

She was standing outside a San Francisco automated public toilet – one of those APTS with the door-lock timers and wash-cycle cleaning. Gordon is director of policy and communications for San Francisco Public Works and her boss, Mohammed Nuru, was doing a television interview about the toilet. 'There was a guy, thirty feet away, passed out drunk against a fence. And he woke up, confused, and decided that he was going to pee. Without getting up.' As Gordon, her boss, and the camera crew stood there, the man's urine flowed through his clothes in a stream toward them, trickling down the sidewalk directly in front of the APT. It was an eye-opener for Gordon, showing her that providing sanitation isn't only about access. It's about culture, habit, and understanding. 'People not only need the bathrooms, [they need to know] they are available. That they don't have to do that anymore.'

Spend even a day or two in San Francisco, a city of 865,000, and you can't avoid homelessness. Its presence is profound. There are dozens of people camped out on the streets of the Tenderloin district, where I stayed for almost a week in spring 2017, working on a radio documentary for the Canadian Broadcasting Corporation about some of the crises facing public bathroom advocates in the US. Around my hotel, on Polk Street near Eddy, and very near the rightfully coveted tables at Brenda's French Soul Food, I did not text and walk; I kept my eyes on the sidewalk for poop and puddles. Even in San Francisco's toniest districts, one advocate for housing and sanitation agreed, the smell of urine can emanate from the sewer grates. There's just so much of it draining in off the streets, she told me. I'm no weak-gutted flower, but I found myself mouth-breathing.

Some organizations say the street population in San Francisco is as high as 10,000; most cite a count of 7,500. About half sleep rough, living completely unsheltered on the streets. The rest live in single-occupancy hotels, stay overnight in shelters, or couch-surf. None of these options provides places where people can hang out during the day. So some folks dehydrate themselves in order to pee less. Some hold in their urine and feces. Both these temporary fixes can lead to serious health conditions. The other solution is to relieve themselves on the streets. Illegally dumped feces are so common in San Francisco – or, perhaps, the city administration is so fundamentally keyed in to the problem – that the public works department maintains a sort of map. Of street poop. To compile the 'poop count,' as Gordon calls it, an employee walks every block of the Tenderloin, a low-income San Francisco neighbourhood where many of the city's single-occupancy hotels lie, noting deposits of feces and making a judgment call on the source

– dog or human. The department then combines those numbers with data from calls for street steam-cleaning to the city's customer service centre to determine the areas of highest need.

And the need is high. At a budget town hall in the Tenderloin in the spring of 2014, Gordon and Nuru heard from a group of middle-schoolers who had come to tell them about the urine puddles and piles of human feces they had to navigate on their way to school. 'These are kids who are already living in a difficult experience, difficult neighbourhood,' says Gordon, 'and one of the first things they have to do in the morning is look out for where they step.' Indeed, during the first six months of 2015, 58 percent of requests for street cleaning were for feces. Five percent for urine. That's a lot of people using the streets as a toilet. As an aside, Rachel Gordon told me that I could make my own poop map if I wanted, using the search function on the City and County of San Francisco's open data site. I suppose anyone could do the same for any jurisdiction with open data. If that's the kind of thing someone's into. Which, I have to say, I absolutely am.

The surprise for most people learning about the abundance of out-of-place poop is that cities in the US, and in other developed nations, have open defecation problems at all.

In fact, San Francisco is not alone. Two bathrooms are being constructed along a stretch of Highway 1 in Big Sur, California, because so many tourists were defecating along the road. In Sacramento, city staff have recommended increasing funding to provide more crews to scrub human poop from sidewalks. And those are just two examples from a single state. Nevertheless, street shit is seen exclusively as a scourge of the developing world. And, well, *of course* it's seen that way. Everybody knows that developed nations – and certainly major cities in the US and Canada – have no shortage of toilets. There are oodles of them. In every building. But here's another sanitation similarity between developed nations and developing ones: it's not simply the *existence* of toilets that solves the problem of open defecation. It's the impact of culture that makes a difference.

There's an unspoken truth that people who are perceived as homeless, or who generally don't fit the norms of mainstream culture, are frequently refused access to customer bathrooms in restaurants, cafés, or shopping malls. A woman pulling a shopping cart containing all her worldly belongings cannot, often, find welcome in an upscale shopping centre bathroom. She can't necessarily afford to buy a coffee or a muffin to gain customer access at a restaurant. Culture is the barrier. But there's also a second way culture, and habit, impact people's toileting, just as they do in India, where those many Swachh Bharat–aided households with new toilets still have family members going to the roadside or field to relieve themselves. It's this: bathrooms aren't always seen as places to go to the bathroom. Let me explain.

San Francisco has twenty-five APTS. They are known, colloquially, as 'JCDecauxs,' after their Paris-based multinational manufacturer, JCDecaux. San Francisco installed its JCDecauxs beginning in the mid-1990s, as part of a scheme that has played out in dozens of US cities. In brief: a media company pays to install and maintain the bathrooms, usually along with an army of matching city-wide 'street furniture' – info kiosks, bus shelters, and the like – in exchange for a portion of the revenue from ads they are plastered with. The specifics are different for every city: some agreements include bike racks and trash bins, others exclude ads on specific street furniture or in specific neighbourhoods, and not every contract is with JCDecaux; but in all cases these are long-term municipal deals that, as the first wave of 1990s-era multi-decade agreements are being renewed, generate into the billions in profit-sharing. The problem is, the toilets can, and do, end up misused and avoided.

Seattle, to cite the most notorious example, in 2008 removed its fleet of five automated public toilets and sold them on eBay; there had been escalating problems of drug use, sex work, and so much garbage being left behind that the automated floor-sweeping mechanisms were repeatedly jammed. In Seattle's case, a law restricting certain outdoor advertising prohibited the usual cost-sharing arrangement, so the city had forked over the full cost of purchasing and installing the bathrooms at the outset – $1 million each. The starting bid on eBay four years later was just $89,000 apiece. In San Francisco, too, Gordon says, many JCDecauxs were being used for drugs, sex, and sleeping. The one located half a block away from city hall, she says, wasn't something she would ever have used herself while, say, out on a lunch break or on her way to or from work. 'I would walk by it several times a day and you would hear anything from two to four people in there.' It's different from a toilet being used as a chicken coop, shrine, or storeroom, but it's the same outcome. These are toilets, but because of their surrounding culture, they're also not toilets.

Then – a change. The Pit Stop.

The Pit Stop is not merely a toilet, but a model of toilet provision. I don't mean to sound highfalutin – some Pit Stops are nothing more than portable toilets that have been trucked to the places the San Francisco poop map has flagged as highest need; others are permanent APTs. What all Pit Stops share are dog waste stations, needle disposal units, and compost, recycling, and landfill bins. But what makes Pit Stops stand out is an audaciously simple concept: they are staffed. That's it. Attendants, former state prisoners who are paid up to sixteen dollars an hour, stand outside the toilets and monitor their use. They say hello to users as they arrive, maintain the queue, and ensure that only one person goes in at a time. After five minutes, they do a courtesy knock. After every use, they make sure that there is no toilet paper or trash on the floor, the toilets are clean and unclogged, and there's soap and paper towels. Those are only the pro forma duties. At the San Francisco Pit Stops I've visited, attendants struck up conversations – just chatting because I was there, not because they knew I was a toilet journalist. They made me feel welcome to the city. The Pit Stop model applies to eighteen toilets in nine neighbourhoods where the most problems were occurring, including the JCDecaux near city hall, which Gordon is now happy to use. I visited it twice, on the way to and from Gordon's city hall office. Pretty nice.

It appears other people are now using these toilets, too. Staffing toilets through the Pit Stop program has seen usage surge. At one location near the San Francisco Civic Center, the number of monthly flushes went from about five hundred to nearly six thousand. These staffed toilets are not used only by homeless people with limited access to indoor bathrooms, but also by tourists, families with young children, and other people with unconventional bathroom needs (Gordon's example is Uber drivers). The city is negotiating a new contract with JCDecaux that's expected to make more Pit Stops available over the coming years.

What's perhaps an even bigger testament to the culture shift happening around these toilets – that people are recognizing Pit Stops as safe, clean, comfortable bathrooms – is the case of the Crookedest Street in the World. That's the nickname of a one-block, brick-paved section of San Francisco's Lombard Street, famous for its eight hairpin turns and robust, year-round tourist presence. The Crookedest Street in the World is in the swanky Russian Hill neighbourhood and boasts some of the city's most expensive real estate. There is no visible homeless population there, no obvious drug problem, no open sex trade. And no bathrooms. Gordon says some residents have asked the city to bring in a Pit Stop.

I have to hand it to San Francisco Public Works. Gordon is a compelling voice for her department – a former journalist, she possesses a credible mix of realism and tiny-steps-matter optimism. And that's impressive in the face of needing to provide toilet service to one of the US's highest per capita homeless populations by way of twenty-five JCDecauxs and a handful of trucked-around porta-potties. But listen. Here's a bigger challenge: how do homeless San Franciscans get clean in a city where bricks-and-mortar drop-in centres provide only an estimated sixteen shower stalls for the ten thousand of them? The answer: Lava Mae.

Lava Mae is a mobile hygiene service. The idea was cooked up by the non-profit's founder, Doniece Sandoval, who wondered, *If the food truck industry can put a gourmet kitchen on wheels, why can't I do it with showers and toilets?* Where most well-meaning people would quickly move on to wondering what to have for dinner or how to entice the kids to turn off the lights when they leave a room, Sandoval set to the task of persuading the city to donate to Lava Mae four decommissioned San Francisco Municipal Transportation Agency buses. One launched in June 2014, another in September 2015 – each with two private Lava Mae compartments, comprising a shower, changing area, toilet, and sink. The retrofit designers retained the wheelchair lifts on the buses' front doors, so those units were wheelchair accessible. Conversion cost just under $100,000 for each vehicle. There was talk, early on, of removing the toilets to squeeze in a third shower compartment. The benefit: an extra shower, plus avoiding having to hold, transport, and dispose of raw sewage. But when the Lava Mae team consulted with community members, they were reminded of an important fact. The first thing most people do before taking a shower? Use the toilet. And, as the Lava Mae team knew well, the toilets their guests had access to were few and far between.

In 2016, Lava Mae added two three-compartment mobile shower trailers, which are less expensive to run and easier to hook up in most-needed areas. The Lava Mae fleet is painted with giant water drops in bright colours. The interiors are baby blue, with large skylights, full-length mirrors, hair dryers, and piped-in music. Towels, shampoo, soap – anything someone might need to get ready for the day, even clean clothes – are provided, and the units undergo a complete cleaning between guests. I got a tour of one outside the main branch of the San Francisco Public Library while I was researching my radio documentary, nipping in quickly between guests at one of Lava Mae's monthly pop-up care villages, where guests can also access dental checkups, haircuts, ID-replacement help, and free lunch. Lava Mae still uses its original buses, and has added trailer units in Silicon Valley and Los Angeles.

Lava Mae's unique guiding doctrine embraces 'radical hospitality,' Sandoval told me after my tour. The people who use Lava Mae's services are referred to as guests, not clients. And they are 'moving through homelessness,' not homeless. 'And they have names,' says Leah Filler, Lava Mae's director of global community engagement. 'They aren't numbers. They aren't tickets.' Those names, I learned at the pop-up village, are known and used. Guests sign up for Lava Mae just like they would get a reservation at a restaurant or a slot at a hair salon. They're given an appointment and they're free to go and get other things done and come back when it's their time. 'That is where the dignity is,' says Filler. 'We believe that the design of a space can reflect the value of the people that use it. So we opted to design something that was high-end and that was beautiful and made just for this community. A community that usually gets nothing but cast-offs.'

Or gets ignored. Filler says hygiene help for the homeless is often an afterthought. Support agencies focus on food, jobs, housing, and health, not on how challenging it can be to keep yourself clean on the streets. 'I have seen women coming up with period stains running down their legs,' Filler says. She has also seen a woman run out of a drop-in resource centre and squat down next to a car – there was a bathroom lineup and she couldn't hold it. (Rachel Gordon confirms, by looking at call centre data and the street poop data, that the most common place for people to defecate outside in San Francisco is in a doorway or between two parked cars.) 'Sometimes we will be cleaning the shower after someone has used it,' says Filler, 'and there will be feces all over the floor. Not because they have relieved themselves, but because it's coming off their clothes and their body.' It's difficult to prioritize showering over food, jobs, housing, and health, but hygiene, clearly, is part of the puzzle. Someone specked with feces 'can't sit on a bus, or walk into a café. There's no way they are going to be able to use a public restroom anywhere. It's just a massive, debilitating, shameful experience that makes people go inward and retreat, isolate themselves, make themselves ill, and put themselves and others at risk.' Another angle to the travesty? 'Right now,' says Filler, 'we are sitting in one of the most affluent cities on the entire planet.' On an early-morning walk I took to San Francisco's Union Square to check out the APT there, scores of people in sleeping bags lay on cardboard boxes in the adjacent doorways of stores like Tiffany & Co., Gucci, Prada, Louis Vuitton, and Bulgari. Silicon Valley's wealth looms in the air over San Francisco like a mist of fine perfume. And there it is again – we don't think of the developed world as a place where people defecate on the edge of the street. And we certainly don't think it's happening in marquee cities like San Francisco.

While Rachel Gordon says there aren't statistics on whether Lava Mae's work has contributed to a reduction in open defecation, requests for steam cleaning have decreased in the areas around Pit Spot locations, and, in the Tenderloin district, incidents have gone down 50 percent. As for the Pit Stops themselves, the cost for running each location is around $100,000 a year, but Gordon says no one's blanching. Elected officials, police, convention and visitors bureaus, local businesses, cleaning crews, non-profits? There's been little push-back. 'Is $100,000-plus too much to spend on one toilet?' Gordon asks. 'I am very, very comfortable as a policy director for my department saying that it's not.' Other cities have heard about the Pit Stop model and she knows of about ten that are adopting it, including Miami, Denver, Los Angeles, and Honolulu.

Pit Stops are revolutionary, sure. But they're a little bit back to the future, too. 'I don't know what it was like in Canada,' says Gordon, 'but growing up in the United States, when I was a kid, the train station bathrooms had attendants, the hotels had them, some of the nicer restaurants had them.' I ask Gordon how she feels about her department's work, which, in my research, is far beyond the norm. 'I don't know if it's mind-blowing and progressive, but–' she pauses, '–it's simple.' That may be, yet public toilets don't come up much at city council meetings in most other cities, if my Google Alerts are to be trusted. And when they do, it's often with acrimony and protest. Public bathrooms seem merely a line item in the budget to be reduced or deleted. The social benefits remain untallied, the financial return uncounted.

New York may think of itself as the capital of the world, but it hasn't yet mastered the art of the public bathroom. Ask Fran Reiter why, and she'll tell you: political fear. Street furniture franchises in New York have ruined careers, so politicians are understandably twitchy about public bathroom contracts. And it was into this political environment that Reiter was appointed deputy mayor by then mayor-elect Rudy Giuliani in 1993.

Reiter sits in a meeting room at her consulting firm, RG Group, at One Penn Plaza. She's agreed to sit down and help me understand why New York has so few public bathrooms on its sidewalks. Truth be told, I'm still wondering, as I sit and take in the thirty-sixth-floor view of the Hudson River behind her, how I got this meeting. 'I don't know anything about you,' Reiter says, right off. 'I just like to talk about toilets.' *Kindred spirit*, I murmur to myself. As it turns out, Reiter and I have other things in common: I never realized I gave a rat's ass about public bathrooms before I had kids; and before she became one of Giuliani's four first-term deputy mayors and got the assignment to fix New York's public toilet situation, Reiter had no passion for them either. She worked the file tirelessly for three years. 'Do I think it's the most important thing that New York government has to deal with? Of course not. But it seems to me it shouldn't be this hard. It's good for the city's economy. It's good from a social standpoint.' Did you catch that? Good for the city's economy? That's a check mark. Reiter started out as deputy mayor for planning and community relations. As her term continued, she ditched the community relations gig and picked up economic development, which Reiter knew was in lockstep with getting public bathrooms in place.

Her boss Giuliani's predecessor, David Dinkins, had tried to get public bathrooms on New York streets from the time his term started in 1990. His focus was easing the frequency of street urination. The administration signed a contract with the German company Wahl for twenty APTs, as per the usual agreement: the company would pay to install and maintain the toilets in exchange for a cut of the revenue from street furniture advertising. The deal ended up enmeshed in a lawsuit because the proposed APTs were not wheelchair accessible. And just like that, the Dinkins deal was dead.

The motivation for Giuliani, who took office January 1, 1994, was quality of life, in Reiter's words. Making the city a better place to live in and visit was a contentious hallmark of Giuliani's mayoralty, from moving porn theatres out of Times Square to cracking down on subway turnstile jumping. Reiter says it's the habit of New Yorkers to suss things out and make them work, and for a long time that's what she and everyone else did when it came to public bathrooms: 'You figure out which department store to go into to use the bathroom.' After she took over the toilet file, she started thinking differently about that make-do approach, and began wondering seriously what tourists – and others – were doing when they had to go. Reiter says 'every New Yorker knows' that if you go through the main floor of the Tiffany & Co. flagship store on Fifth Avenue and head upstairs at the back, you can go into the bathroom. But, she adds, 'you know as well as I do that if some homeless person, some bag lady, walks into Tiffany's, they are not going to let her use the toilet.'

As Reiter worked on a request for proposals for a street furniture contract – including coordinated bus-stop shelters, newsstands, advertising kiosks, and public bathrooms – she started to hear opposition. The Dinkins accessibility snag was solved, after several manufacturers designed bathrooms small enough to fit on New York sidewalks and big enough to be wheelchair compatible. But there were new rumblings. Community groups worried the bathrooms would become crime hubs. The newsstand owners opposed any shift in the status quo, because their stands were licensed to them by the city at low cost under long-standing contracts. Eventually, Reiter came to an agreement with the newsstand operators, allowing rebuilding and rebranding of existing stands, and she felt confident that nighttime closures and automation would keep the bathrooms clean and safe. But the biggest challenge? 'People want toilets; they don't want ads.'

But without the ads, the business case evaporates. Reiter ballparks it: every public bathroom needs the revenue from three advertising kiosks to cover the cost of installation and maintenance. Reiter later discovered this had been another Dinkins snarl – citizens were so opposed to the advertising kiosks, the administration felt forced to propose a one-to-one ratio of toilets to kiosks. Wahl had been the only bidder, and in fact the company pulled out after it won because the one-to-one ratio meant there wasn't enough money in it. Reiter wouldn't repeat that mistake in her request for proposals. The final hurdle was the last piece of the puzzle necessary to make the business case successful: the need to award the furniture contract to a single vendor.

It's rare for a large-scale municipal project to be covered by one contract awarded to one company. And especially when it's such a massive amount of money – back in the mid-1990s, when it was Reiter's baby, the street furniture contract was worth around $500 million and covered all five boroughs. That kind of cash makes politicians nervous. It's much safer to break a contract into smaller pieces, covering smaller areas and spreading the wealth among several bidders. That way, a hitch means only part of the deal is at risk, and there's less likelihood of being accused of directing a swimming pool of money to your friends. But there was no way to break up the street furniture contract. The money for toilets in lower-density areas was going to have to come from ads in high-density areas. Basically, Manhattan was the economic driver. If the boroughs were divvied up and a company won only, say, Staten Island, Queens, or even downtown Brooklyn, the ad revenue wouldn't be enough. 'If you didn't win Manhattan, you were dead.' So, one vendor it was. Reiter got the request for proposals approved in 1996 – in case you're not counting, it took three years.

Perhaps inevitably, accusations of favouritism swirled around the deal before it was even awarded. Reiter left her deputy mayorship in 1997 to manage Giuliani's successful re-election campaign. Soon after he won and Reiter had moved on, the mayor killed the toilet scheme. Reiter says he was looking ahead to his next political move – president, or at least governor. 'His political advisors came back to him and told him, "You should find a way to get out of this. It is going to come back and bite you in the ass."' Instead, it bit Reiter and never let go. She went on to head up the New York Convention and Visitors Bureau, the city's official marketing and tourism agency, and to work as executive deputy director of state operations for New York governor Andrew Cuomo. But she's still got a public bathroom policy hangover. 'My interest in tourism and that part of the economic development of the city was my life for a long period of time,' she says. 'The lack of facilities for visitors to the city is a real issue. It's bad. How can you be the capital of the world and not [provide] a place to pee?'

Giuliani's successor, Michael Bloomberg, managed to get a new street furniture plan rolling, even adding sheltered bike parking to the mix, along with the promise of twenty automated pay toilets. At this point – a decade after Reiter got her request for proposals approved – the twenty-year contract, covering all five boroughs, was worth one billion dollars. The city signed with Spanish company Cemusa in 2006, and Reiter's political fear narrative began playing out immediately, with two rival bidders, including JCDecaux, filing lawsuits against the city with allegations of favouritism. Bloomberg would become the fourth successive New York mayor whose administration was accused of this kind of street furniture corruption. The contract survived into Mayor Bill de Blasio's first term, but so far, Cemusa has installed only five of the twenty planned APTs – one at Corona Plaza in Queens, one at Fordham Plaza in the Bronx, one at La Plaza de las Americas in Washington Heights, one in Midtown

Manhattan's Madison Square Park, and another, which has been out of order every damn time I've visited it, at Grand Army Plaza in Brooklyn. That leaves scant time to install the remaining fifteen APTs before the contract expires in 2026. Cemusa, meanwhile, has been acquired by its rival JCDecaux. It's like a toilet soap opera.

Twenty-eight years since Dinkins. Five toilets installed. Reiter shakes her head. 'If the city is not going to do it, you have to find another way to solve the problem.'

It's early January 2015, in Manhattan. But at the Herald Square and Greeley Square public bathrooms, Christmas is still hanging around. The oval-shaped buildings are lush with evergreens and red berries. Each sits at a far end of two treed plazas in Midtown Manhattan: the Herald Square toilet bordering 34th Street, the Greeley Square one on 32nd. The honking, talking, and clanking of the city surrounds these bathrooms; the plazas form a bowtie-shaped valley beneath mountains of grey mid-rises and the fire-engine red of the Macy's flagship sign. The dark-green pods are pretty little oases. Inside: white tile, mosaic ceilings, and fresh lilies in wall-mounted glass vases. These free bathrooms are open daily at eight in the morning until nine at night and welcome a steady flow of users. Also, they're immaculate. John Glenn (the guy who supervises sanitation at Herald and Greeley Squares, not the late astronaut) points to a worker wielding a spray bottle and mop who runs back and forth all day between the bathrooms, cleaning them. 'All public park restrooms should be very clean,' Glenn says. 'But you go in some of them? And they are not.'

Glenn sometimes oversees the public bathroom at Bryant Park, which he says people call the cleanest in the city. I'm with him. It might be the loveliest, too. The *Village Voice* once said these free public bathrooms meet a 'nearly absurd standard of excellence.' As hundreds skate to Louis Armstrong at Bryant Park's 42nd Street outdoor rink, I nip over to a stately one-storey 1911 granite building in the park's corner. Inside the main door sits an urn with a two-metre-high spray of fresh flowers. The counters are marble; the music, Vivaldi (Dan Biederman, the president of the Bryant Park Corporation, which manages the park, will tell me later that there were many meetings to discuss the music – the relative merits of different genres and the volume). The attendant stands smiling near the hand dryer as I wash up. I thank her, and comment on the cleanliness. 'What you could do,' she says, 'is go to the website and let them know. Tell them you spoke to Rosanna.' I did.

These bathrooms – paragons of their species – are maintained by Business Improvement Districts. BIDS are consortiums of businesses or commercial property owners who fund projects in their areas, separate from or on top of standard city services. They might pay for street cleaning, security, or planter boxes. The idea is to make an area more pleasant in order to bring in more people. Herald Square and Greeley Square are run by the 34th Street Partnership; Bryant Park, by the Bryant Park Corporation. The two BIDS share a management team. They also share a philosophy – there's a financial return on nice public toilets.

This hasn't always been the vision. Bryant Park, which had been a reliable refuge for New Yorkers since the late nineteenth century, fell into neglect in the 1970s. The 1980s were a decade of resurgence, and after a four-year renewal, the park reopened in 1991. But it wasn't until 2006 that a $200,000 bathroom renovation brought the public toilets to their current level of luxury. A more recent renovation, completed in 2017 at a cost of $280,000, has jacked these bathrooms up a notch higher. As it happens, Herald and Greeley Squares briefly boasted New York's first APTS in 2001. They mostly worked, and were, in a world of few other options, used. 'It wasn't a bad experience,' Biederman, who also runs these bathrooms, told the *New York Times*. 'It just wasn't a great experience, and we wanted it to be great.' They closed the automated units in 2008 and converted them to the manually cleaned über-toilets they are today. They reopened in 2009 and usage increased fivefold in the first year.

The BIDS *get* public bathrooms. For them, it's obvious. So why not for everyone else? 'It's a no-brainer,' says Reiter. 'It's a quality-of-life issue. We don't live in the Third World here. We are in New York City.'

5

KICKING UP A STINK

Joan Kuyek was protesting on Parliament Hill in Ottawa when she felt a familiar urge. She had to go to the bathroom. She looked past the crowds and placards and took in a familiar sight beyond the Gothic revival architecture and the eternal flame where tourists sit for holiday snaps: no public toilets. Kuyek had never imagined herself as a campaigner for the right to relieve herself. But it hit her in that moment – this was Canada's capital city, the seat of its national government. There were hundreds of people enjoying the right to peaceful protest and there wasn't a toilet to be had. She found out later that there's a john cloistered behind parliament's west block. (A classic public toilet story: I have been in and out of Ottawa my entire life, visiting and living there. I had no idea this bathroom existed until Kuyek told me.) Kuyek had lived in Ottawa for fifteen years by that time and had lobbied extensively on the Hill, mostly in her former role as national coordinator of MiningWatch Canada. She, like me, had no idea it existed. It was her legs-crossed breaking point. She knew something needed to be done. Except, she thought, 'Who wants to spend their life being the toilet lady?'

Joan Kuyek, it turns out.

A few years later, Kuyek saw the plans for phase one of Ottawa's light rail transit system. And, in them, she saw a problem – too few public bathrooms. The $2.1-billion LRT will ferry eleven thousand passengers an hour in each direction when it launches in late 2018. In the initial plans, there were public bathrooms only at the two ends of the new east-west line, twelve and a half kilometres and thirteen stops apart – the minimum number required under the Ontario Building Code. Kuyek put herself to the task of lobbying for more. 'Low-hanging fruit,' she called it. 'So obvious.'

Phase two, coming in 2021, announced extensions heading farther east and west, as well as south, and more than forty new kilometres and twenty-three additional stops at a projected cost of $3.6 billion. The public bathroom upshot? Three more end-of-line toilets, as per the building code. Kuyek asks a salient question: what if you're not starting at the start or ending at the end? Because, let's face it, without enough public toilets, the lines won't be much good to any commuter who needs to use the bathroom, which, at one point or another, is *every* commuter.

Fewer and fewer subway and commuter rail stations in North America have open bathrooms. New York maintained more than 1,500 subway station toilets in the 1940s; today there are estimated to be around seventy-five. Toronto has eleven public bathrooms in its seventy-five-station subway system, all in fare-paid areas the general public walking by cannot get into. Transit authorities often cite security fears as the reason for eliminating public bathrooms at station stops. But that's a snake eating its tail – bathrooms are not checked enough during non-peak times, they end up misused, they get closed. The cycle would stop if bathrooms were better maintained, and attended to, and used more, as we've seen with the Pit Stop model in San Francisco. The next old chestnut is cost – during a 2015 debate about the LRT, Ottawa City Councillor Jan

Harder said the city has enough budget items to juggle already, and adding public bathrooms to the mix is too much.

Kuyek wasn't having any of it. She gathered together nine activist friends, launched a campaign called GottaGo!, and prepared for a journey to bathroom justice. Stop one: calling bullshit on the security-risk argument. Bathrooms are often cast as hot spots for anti-social behaviour like illegal drug use, public sex, or sleeping. But instead of putting users and passersby at risk, Kuyek argues, public bathrooms bring in more people, who keep watch over public spaces. She says the real hazards are for the people using public bathrooms to sleep or self-medicate. 'Someone who is shooting up isn't going to be dangerous to me,' the seventy-five-year-old says. 'They are a danger to themselves.' And cost? Sure. Bathrooms cost money. Ottawa explored charging a fee to help cover its LRT public bathrooms. The idea was pooh-poohed by members of the public and the city backed down. Kuyek knows that, ultimately, getting bathrooms in transit stops isn't life-or-death. But it is life, clearly. Quality of life. 'The natural human urge to defecate and urinate,' she says, 'shouldn't be a barrier to people using different parts of the city.'

Ah, but it is.

Kuyek knows a lot of people who already don't go downtown because there are no solid options for number two. And the new, soon-to-open LRT stations may not be adequately dousing anyone's fear of being caught short. Imagine a commute from one of the rural communities outside Ottawa. You finish breakfast and a coffee and head out. You drive to a park-and-ride to leave your car. No toilets. You get on the LRT at one of the bathroomless stops. No toilets. You walk from your bathroomless destination stop to work or get on a bus. No toilets. Where – and when, finally – do you get to use the washroom? Toilet researchers talk about commuters 'chaining' trips – you grab milk on the way home from work at a convenience store, collect your kid from daycare, and hit the bakery for morning croissants. It's sensible, efficient errand-running. But it also adds time to the trip home. And jacks up the likelihood that you will need a bathroom. Not allowing for that inevitability in an urban core is 'organized irresponsibility,' Kuyek says.

Though Ottawa, to an extent, has come around. There will be extra public bathrooms added 'at the request of Council for passengers' convenience,' according to Steve Cripps, the project's construction director. That's an extra two bathrooms on the original new line, and another pair on phase two – all at major transit points where people are most likely to get on or off the system or transfer to a bus. The biggest coup, to my mind, is a public bathroom that's being added at the far-south Earl Armstrong/Bowesville Station. It's not required under the building code and it's not at a high-volume station either, but it's nevertheless been approved. Project planner Chris Swail says that 'staff recommend that Earl Armstrong/Bowesville station be treated as any other terminus station and be fit up with public washrooms.' In other words: people will probably need a bathroom at that stop, so let's go ahead and plan to put one in.

Call it a win for the livable city.

The 'livable city' (and its jargon-mates, the healthy city, the walkable city, and the age-friendly city) is the contemporary mantra in planning circles. Livability includes the ideas that the best cities are ones where people can easily connect with each other and their environments, where people can walk or use public transit to get them where they need to go, and where people can access urban green spaces for leisure and exercise. Livability can be literally quantified – an idea that originated in the 1980s, as a way for corporations and governments to rate how much extra to pay employees to work in inhospitable places. It's since done a one-eighty, becoming a way of measuring how *good* places are to settle down in. Urban parks and fast, efficient public transit networks move a city up the livability ladder; sprawl, pollution, and congestion move a city down.

Livability and an abundance of free, clean, accessible public bathrooms should go hand in hand. It's not that those who calculate livability – journalists and researchers from magazines like *Forbes*, the *Economist*, and *Monocle* – need to be out counting toilets. It's that public facilities like restrooms provide an urban support structure for a good city. The ticks on the livability checklist have nothing to do with bathrooms *directly*, but much, indeed, to do with them *indirectly*. Public bathrooms are all about mobility. They're a tool that allows people to move around the city, to stay later and longer, and to go farther.

Bathroom author Barbara Penner has a genius example. She was thrilled when the popular planning murmur turned to livability, because public conveniences like toilets play into the concept so soundly. 'So obvious,' she thought (just like Joan Kuyek with the LRT bathrooms; great toilet minds think alike). The gleam came off the porcelain when Penner was at a healthy cities conference organized by the *Lancet*, the world's pre-eminent medical journal. Active transportation – getting people off their duffs and walking, skateboarding, or cycling to work, school, and on errands – was heavy on the agenda. Not a soul mentioned public bathrooms. Not even in passing. Not even once. 'Surely, if you want people to spend an hour walking to and from work,' Penner says, 'you should be thinking about that. Still, totally off the radar.'

Is it the utter plainness of public toilets that allows us to so easily forget them? Kuyek tells me that when she was in the process of getting signatures for a petition to amend the original Ottawa LRT design, people were dumbstruck that bathrooms weren't just automatically part of the city's plan. But a municipal councillor Kuyek approached about the matter was surprised in an entirely different way. The councillor was shocked she was inquiring about bathrooms. The city had managed without them for decades, she told Kuyek, so why bother now? Well, because every time Kuyek raised the issue at a public event, at least two people – often more – came up afterward to thank her. 'People have been living with the shame and the need for so long,' she says. 'They just haven't been able to give voice to it.'

According to Robert Brubaker, co-founder of the American Restroom Association, livability is about all the things that allow people to get out and use their cities. And it has as much to do with pee and poo as it does with lighting, benches, and on-time buses. Brubaker calls public toilets part of the commons, along with street lamps, sidewalks, and roads – segments of the urban environment we expect governments to provide to every citizen using shared tax dollars.

'The commons' is something of an antiquated term, evoking grazing sheep and Old Europe's squares, but it connects well to modern city life. The urban commons are shared resources, plain and simple. When the commons work best, we almost don't notice they're there. We have places to walk where we need to walk, and places to sit where we enjoy sitting and socializing. Bathrooms into which we hurry with our about-to-pee-her-pants three-year-old. Travelled spaces are lit, trash finds its way easily into bins, and swings for kids are never far. The commons are for anyone and everyone, for free. The small-scale infrastructure of the living, breathing city.

But urban commons are shrinking. This can happen literally – for instance, when green spaces are cleaved off for parking. But often – and more subtly – it's about ownership and stewardship. An example: Herald Square and Greeley Square in Midtown

Manhattan are the property of New York City. But they are managed by the 34th Street Partnership, a private, not-for-profit management company. Don't get me wrong – they are lovely public spaces, well-maintained and full of planters and trees and tables and chairs and monuments. (And, as we've heard, they have some of the nicest, cleanest free public washrooms in Manhattan.) But all these perks aren't strictly for the satisfaction of any citizen strolling by. The parks' provision and management work to the advantage of businesses in the area.

The question is: does it matter?

Does it matter who provides benefits, so long as those benefits are there for whoever needs them? Some people say yes, it does. If a piece of architecture or infrastructure is in the commons, then any citizen has a right to it – but if it's in the hands of a private enterprise, then its use becomes a privilege. Access can be granted. Access can be denied.

Public bathrooms aren't always seen as automatic for the people. And this has everything to do with how they are defined. It seems a simple question: what's a public bathroom? But nothing's ever simple on this topic.

There are two essential but divisive concepts here: public bathrooms and publicly accessible bathrooms. They are different. And it's helpful, from a public bathroom policy perspective, to know which kind of bathroom you want to back. Brubaker is firmly on the side of the former. Public bathrooms, he says, are facilities that are open year-round, seven days a week, and without admission cost. They can be free-standing, or they can be in public buildings, like subway stations. Café and mall bathrooms only count if their availability to the public is clearly advertised. A pointed nod here to bathrooms in municipal public libraries, which, in most cities I've been to, function beautifully as welcoming public spaces. It's all about intention. Brubaker's kind of public bathrooms are public because they exist for anyone's use, no strings attached. They don't exist to serve the occupants of buildings who are there primarily for other reasons, like shopping, or viewing art, or working, or eating. 'If you walk into a Walmart, and you are legitimately in there,' he says, 'you should be able to use the restroom, but it's not a public restroom.'

John Griggs, a UK plumbing consultant and wastewater engineer based in the north of London, is on the second side of the debate. His toilet claim to fame is his long-time work developing British and European standards for sanitary provision. Need to know how to make a bathroom work right? Ask John Griggs. But don't ask him to buy into Brubaker's nuanced definitions of public toilets. He doesn't care who maintains a bathroom or where it is – as long as the public can use it, it's public. 'Nobody cares who owns it,' he says. 'They want the facilities.' Griggs is right, to a point. Most of us just want a bathroom when we need to go. We don't care if it's outside city hall or inside Boston Pizza. Of course, Boston Pizza cares, because Boston Pizza pays for the toilet paper and the water and the cost of the employee who must clean the place. And while for Boston Pizza there's an almost guaranteed pay-off – people shelling out their bucks for Kick'n Memphis Chicken and Bud Light – what about the situation inside, say, public libraries? Those are some of the most-used bathrooms for the public in many downtown cores. And the librarians who work there have to stickhandle scads of people using these spaces and, crucially, the messes they make. The return on investment in this case isn't quite the same.

But these clashing definitions show something about the place of toilets in our city-psyches. Most of us have been conditioned not to expect public bathrooms as part of the urban package deal, like we do benches and green spaces and monuments. But imagine if we relied on local businesses to provide our street lights and sidewalks, out of the goodness of their corporate hearts or, more realistically, in order to ensure sufficient foot traffic to sell enough widgets to pay the rent. That would seem out of whack. But with toilets, it doesn't. We've just gotten used to it.

As I've said, I don't know of any statutory requirements in Canada, the US, or the UK for local governments to install on-street toilets for public use. Municipalities provide bathrooms – or don't – at their discretion. This has become the norm in part because of evolving regulations around bathrooms inside buildings. Remember that construction boom of Victorian-era public bathrooms? I've explained the problems with them, including lack of attention to the needs of women, children, and wheelchair users. But they were *something*, right? They spoke to an understanding of public need. Of public provision for public good. For reasons I've already outlined, they've been picked off one by one over the last fifty-odd years. Over the same time span, many jurisdictions started requiring bathrooms in gas stations. (There's a master's thesis in this somewhere – bathrooms for pedestrians being replaced by bathrooms for drivers.) At this same time, through the twentieth century, government regulations requiring bathrooms in all buildings, in numbers matching occupancy, became standard. This sounds good – losing bathrooms in some places but gaining them in many more places. But those replacement johns – in gas stations and stores and office buildings – are the kind Robert Brubaker believes aren't exactly as beneficial as the ones that used to be fixtures on our streets and in our parks. Remember: with public bathrooms, access is a given. With publicly *accessible* bathrooms, access can be granted. Access can also be denied.

One of the hallmark lobbying jobs of the the American Restroom Association has been to beef up access signage requirements – forcing building owners to install signs that indicate where patrons can find toilets and how they can gain entrance when they are locked. 'When you went into a small store,' Brubaker says, 'they would say, "Oh, we don't have customer restrooms," or "We don't have any restrooms." And the fact is, they did. They had to, by the building codes.'

While building codes often favour access, they are usually unknown to the public, unpromoted, and unenforced. In the US, the common transit-system practice of closing down restrooms that's endemic to big-city stations is usually a violation of state building code. And those signage requirements the ARA helped solidify? As with potty-parity regulations, they only apply to new construction or major renovations. In the UK, there are robust standards for how to build the best public bathrooms – and I mean *robust*: the July 2017 British Standards Institution's Guide to Standardization for public toilets alone runs fifty-four pages – but these best-practice standards aren't universally implemented because they are voluntary. If you're looking for the best possible user experience, you build according to standards; if you are looking to get by with the basic, cheapest option that meets the legal requirements for safety and accessibility, you build to code.

It's all so messy – code, depending on the jurisdiction, can work at city, state, provincial, or federal levels. It's overlaid by voluntary standards and the sticky quirkiness of culture and custom. Jo-Anne Bichard calls public bathrooms a layer cake. 'You've got general politics, social politics, you've got economics, you've got ability, you've got the sort of humanness of what we do with our waste products,' she says. Bichard is a design anthropologist who works at the Helen Hamlyn Centre for Design at London's Royal College of Art. 'We go to other countries and they've got a different relationship with shit, and a different relationship to toilets that we sometimes don't understand.' You can't often say the same about sidewalks or garbage cans. But instead of digging into our complex relationships with public bathrooms, instead of really looking at the place where biological need meets culture and striving to get it right, governments too often zip their lips. Planners and committee chairs sound off about the livable, walkable, healthy, age-friendly city. But, somehow, providing a comprehensive network of public bathrooms, in the way cities create spiderwebs of bus routes, parks, and playgrounds, isn't part of that conversation.

Every time Gail Ramster opens a meaty new government report on improving main streets in the UK, the first thing she does is a Control-Find on her keyboard for the word *toilet*. And every time? *NOT FOUND*. I do it, too – every study I pull up. I search *toilet, bathroom, restroom,* and *washroom*. Consider: Ontario's Action Plan for Seniors. I looked at the document in 2013, when it was seven thousand brand-new words. *Toilet? Bathroom? Restroom? Washroom?* Nothing – even though the strategy paper touts the necessity of working toward 'age-friendly communities' and addresses: among other things, transportation, civic participation, and outdoor spaces like walkways, roads, and parks. The updated version from 2017, in front of me as I write this, has one sidebar mention of a $50,000 grant given to a Peterborough, Ontario, organization that has made changes to benefit 'older customers,' including good lighting, wide and clutter-free store aisles, large print signs, and – practically as an after-thought – accessible *washrooms*. How about New Westminster, BC's Livable City Strategy? Nothing. The Downtown Tucson Partnership's revitalization document? One mention in one line about a proposed outdoor-event pavilion redesign. I dunno, pick one yourself, do a search. Let me know if anything toilet-related comes up.

'It's like, really?' Ramster says. 'You know this is important, but you either didn't think about it, or you didn't want to think about it. It's all about hanging baskets and parking.' Ramster is Jo-Anne Bichard's co-researcher at the Royal College of Art. The two have worked together on public toilet projects looking at design and inclusivity, and the fact that when it comes to city infrastructure, public bathrooms are ridiculously overlooked. 'Because they're toilets, people don't make a fuss,' Ramster says. 'But if it were food, if they were cafés, you wouldn't have any of this.'

Ramster confirms my own findings – most politicians don't love to talk toilets. And good bloody luck finding an economist willing to take on a cost-benefit calculation. The argument that people aren't making full use of their cities – less shopping, less going to the theatre, less eating out – because there's limited public toilet access holds water for me, but it's tricky to put into numbers. Much easier to add up the annual maintenance costs of public bathrooms, stick the figures in the loss column, and call it a day. Yet, Bichard and Ramster's interview subjects have told them unequivocally: access to bathrooms affects what parts of the city they visit. An older man in one of their studies told them how he used to like to take the train to the next town. There was a shop there he fancied, and it was a nice little jaunt that kept him moving. But since the toilet at the local train station had closed, he couldn't make it anymore without being uncomfortable or risking an accident. So he just stopped going to the next town. He also stopped spending his money there. 'This is just one person,' says Bichard. She wonders how many millions or billions are being lost from local economies because of the winnowing of public toilets. Ramster has her own example. She used to visit the public bathrooms at Covent Garden, until they were privatized and demanded a fifty-pence charge. She doesn't go anymore.

Ramster is leading the creation of the Great British Public Toilet Map, an online resource that has pulled together data from crowdsourcing and hundreds of local councils. The map pinpoints the location of publicly accessible toilets with notes on whether the bathrooms are gender-free, if they include baby-changing stations, what hours they are open, and what the charge is to enter, if any.

But even without the internet in our purses and pockets, all of us carry around mental maps of our neighbourhoods and of the communities where we visit, work, and shop. We know to go here, and not there, for good coffee. We know where there's a trash bin for dog-poop bags. And we know the spots where we can find a place to have a pee. Mental maps, then, are outlines of the urban commons. Depending on the day and the need, our map controls our movements. One of the women Bichard interviewed described it to her this way: 'I'm like a little animal. I always use the same tracks.'

Some researchers call this the bladder's leash. Take away toilets and the leash gets yanked back. And as the urban commons are depleted – as green spaces shrink, as drinking fountains get turned off, and as public toilets close – our maps get smaller. We adapt: in part because humans are nimble, but also because we don't even realize we're doing it, because the changes happen slowly over time. But all of this, says Bichard, is a harder slog for seniors, who are more likely to deal with incontinence and aging muscles and on whom the little changes can have a far greater effect. 'It's like the bench at the end of your street that you have never sat on,' she says. 'Because all your life you never needed to sit on it. And then suddenly you get to, like, sixty-five or seventy years old and you've got that shopping and it's just that little bit too heavy and, "Oh gosh, the bench is gone! But there was always a bench there!"' When what's missing is a toilet, Bichard says, a lot of older people, especially women, don't want to say anything – it's private. 'And it might also be the realization that they're not going out as much because there aren't toilets, and they don't know how to blame it.'

The City of Toronto in 2013 wrote a massive strategy paper to help prepare it for the unique needs of its exploding population of seniors. The document deals with a smorgasbord of social and physical barriers to the urban world, all collected through talking to seniors and their caregivers. Control-F *toilet, bathroom, restroom, washroom*? Nothing.

I called Dena Warman, then–policy development officer for the city. She told me public bathrooms came up in passing during the consultation phase, but 'not so much in terms of the ongoing needs of a seniors' population.' (When I relate this to Bichard, with her years of experience coaxing details from interviewees about age-friendly toilets, she tells me she suspects no one asked direct questions about public bathroom needs, such as: Would you like this? How about this? 'You're talking about something very, very personal. We don't all sit around talking about what we do in the toilet.') Warman explained that the strategy started with a focus on halting social isolation. But surely, I said, having adequate public bathrooms is a key deterrent against social isolation. Warman paused. Everything in the document, she repeated, ties into pulling seniors into the wider world. She paused again. 'It all makes sense to me when I say that. But when you say that basic infrastructure isn't there, it's like a light bulb.'

Bichard calls it 'like throwing a pebble in a lake.' The range within which people will travel in their city or town starts out wide. As people age, they grow fearful of not reaching the toilet in time, or of finding a toilet they have always visited shuttered. They stop engaging with their community. They stop walking in the park. They lose out on chance encounters with friends and neighbours. Eventually, they stop leaving home all together. They don't stand up and scream that the public toilets have all disappeared. Most don't even share their concerns with friends. 'They go on cruises instead,' Bichard says.

And, actually, Bichard's pebble-in-a-lake comment was one of *my* light-bulb moments. Because that was the situation with me and my three-year-old and baby at the Halifax Common so many years before. Leaving the house was something I needed. Badly. But it was also a test of how far I'd get before something went wrong in the toilet department. The Common was only a couple of blocks from my house. Low stakes, so I was willing to risk it. But what if I felt like going for a coffee, say, which was another kilometre up the road? That was a walk, and an activity, I used to welcome. But not with the kids in tow. With them, I usually just puttered around the Common and headed home. The safer choice.

Robert Brubaker says the American Restroom Association gets emails from young girls who have quit sports teams because schools don't allow them access to bathrooms after hours, and community sports fields have no bathroom facilities or portable toilets. Try changing a tampon discreetly on a soccer pitch. That's fun. Brubaker says boys typically go to the edges of the fields to pee. When girls reluctantly do the same, 'the guys don't all look away; they make catcalls.' An indignity on top of an indignity. The predicament is similar for female runners, who also email the ARA for help.

Start cataloguing the categories of special-needs bathroom users and it hits hard: it's not a question of *which* unique groups need easy access to free public toilets in order to make full use of the city, but, rather, who *doesn't* need such access? Bichard has interviewed close to five hundred public toilet users in her research. She started with people with physical disabilities, then she was talking to women who were pregnant or who had young children. Next, it was teenaged boys who wouldn't use public toilets for fear of being attacked. ('They risk more violence than most people, so they are very concerned that toilets are in a safe place.') Then, teenaged girls who were nervous for the same reason. Seniors joined in, then folks with invisible disabilities like colostomies and urostomies, then menstruating women, and fathers actively partaking in child care who were frustrated by missing changing tables in men's rooms. Apparently special needs aren't so special after all.

Of course, the city is not just a place of living and commuting. It is a workplace, too.

The rights of workers to have bathroom access and break times were enshrined through the toil of the early labour movement starting after the Industrial Revolution. But people who work in mobile professions – truck and delivery drivers, bus and rail operators, mobile librarians, beat cops, postal workers, contractors, and the Uber drivers Rachel Gordon says Pit Stops help in San Francisco, to name a few – can face tricky times finding loos on the move. I asked a former beat cop what he did when he needed to go. Foot patrollers make use of their neighbourhood connections, he told me – they use the bathroom in restaurants, malls, or hotels. They also go back to the station to file paperwork or to eat lunch and go to the restroom there. In emergencies, a patrol car can pick them up. (Police horses, on the other hand? The whole city is their toilet.) After the September 11 attacks in New York, Washington, and Pennsylvania, Robert Brubaker says, a lot of the places where even uniformed bus drivers used to pop out of their vehicles to use the washroom were no longer available to them. For truck drivers, those spots have never existed.

Gillian Kemp isn't a trucker. She's a semi-retired medical appliance company director sitting on an ottoman, in her floral-decorated living room in Hertfordshire, UK. Seven years ago, she was at a highway rest stop and she heard two women truckers talking about how hard it was to find a bathroom. Kemp is nosy (her word). 'Excuse me,' she said. 'Tell me more.' Soon after that conversation, she was heading up Truckers' Toilets UK.

Motorway service stops are convenient places for truck drivers to grab something to eat and use the bathroom, provided the busy highways they're on aren't 'gummed up,' as Kemp puts it, with standstill traffic. But feeder roads leading into large cities don't have those stop spots. As truckers move deeper into urban cores, there's nowhere to park a twelve- to eighteen-foot truck. When drivers deliver goods to companies, they often park in the only urban spots they can legally and physically squeeze into. But they aren't employees of the companies they are delivering to – a driver dropping a skid of Liquid Paper to Walmart works for a shipper or is an independent contractor. So while Walmart is legally obliged to provide bathrooms for its employees, there's no statutory requirement to grant bathroom access to truck drivers pulling up at the bay doors. Check any online trucker chats and you'll quickly find out: from department stores to florists, they are routinely told that employee bathrooms are off limits. None of this changes truckers' biological needs, of course. So in dense urban environments where there's nowhere else to pull over, they make use of two options, both demeaning: hold it or 'bucket and chuck it.'

It takes some manual (and other) dexterity to urinate into a container behind the wheel of a truck. More so for women. But so-called 'trucker bombs' litter highways. One Washington State road-cleaning crew found almost three thousand bottles of urine – mostly four-litre milk jugs – in one year. When those bottles are ripe and solar-heated and a weed-whacker clips them, they can explode. Fines for lobbing them can reach more than a thousand dollars in some US states.

Holding urine might be better for the environment and the road-cleaning crews, but it can elevate blood pressure and boost the likelihood of bladder infections. It's no boon to other drivers either. Kemp mentions a study showing that concentration drops when people can't make it to the bathroom. But truckers, she says, don't like to frame their toilet dilemmas in terms of distracted driving: 'They could lose their jobs.' What can't be held or chucked is menstrual blood. Kemp says some female drivers inject themselves with hormones to stop their periods.

Just imagine any of these solutions applying to the average office worker: 'Sorry, Mildred, you can't leave your cubicle today. Just toss your urine out the window. Hope you aren't on your period. Ta ta.'

Taxi drivers are another breed of mobile worker without johns in their offices. Laura Norén clued in to the issue when she walked up to a cab in New York and her driver was in the midst of peeing into a disposable coffee cup. Norén, a sociologist, has researched the experiences of cabbies as a means of looking at the ways the urban environment fails us. She wrote about the situation in an essay for the collection *Toilet: Public Restrooms and the Politics of Sharing*, a book she co-edited with Harvey Molotch. Norén wanted to tell the story of missing bathrooms through a middle-class lens, so it couldn't be ignored as 'some marginalized, poor people's problem,' as it's often presented when the focus is primarily on the homeless. Even if many taxi drivers are new-immigrant men of colour, Norén told me from her office at NYU, middle- and upper-class urbanites at least interact with cabbies; they pay the homeless (and their toilet problems) 'about as much attention as a bench.'

Norén found that New York cab drivers use the same species of networks as beat cops – making connections in different parts of the city. Crucial difference: the direction cabbies travel is determined by their fares, so the friends-with-bathrooms solution can't work all the time. For her research, Norén would get into random cabs, select a destination, and start talking. She would ask the hardest part of their jobs, hoping they would mention bathrooms. Not one did. They wouldn't touch the topic of toilets without being asked directly. 'Hardest interviews I have ever done,' she said.

Most of the cabbies told Norén the same thing – parking to pee isn't workable. Hourly pay-parking lots bite into profits and taxi queues demand constant movement forward. Illegal street parking fines can go to 115 bucks a pop. And even when cabbies do find a spot to leave their vehicles for a few minutes, there aren't enough on-street public bathrooms. Cafés and restaurants are plastered with customers-only signs. Norén conducted her research in New York, but she believes this urinary quandary holds in the densest places in most major cities. The solution, many drivers admitted, is the same as truckers' – coffee cups, plastic baggies, laundry detergent containers (the choice of the savviest drivers, says Norén, because they're opaque and have a lingering perfumey smell), and water bottles. 'The Poland Spring bottle,' she says, holding one up to her screen cam to show me. 'The mouth is really narrow. But I've seen it a million times, so they must be very skilled.' It's not something drivers want to do, only something they must, which they then get used to. 'You get rid of the coffee cup and it's over.' A degrading part of everyday life.

How is this normal? If access to proper facilities in cities helps everyone, and lack of access harms many, why don't things change? It seems it's at least partly because the mobile workforce doesn't talk openly about its urinary strife. Taxi and truck drivers, bus drivers, and beat cops find ways and make do. There's no fault-finding, and if there is, it's with bodies, not infrastructure – hence female truck drivers artificially stopping menstruation. Seniors play the same game. As we age, we all need to go to the toilet more and we all need to get to facilities faster. 'And we blame that on us,' says Jo-Anne Bichard, 'not on the overlords who provide the services.' (If they do.) A group of women Gail Ramster interviewed take water tablets for high blood pressure, which increases the need to urinate. 'When they are going out for the day, they just don't take them.' They're fixing the problem by trying to fix their bodies. Making do.

Doesn't it seem like public toilets are so undervalued, so easy to ignore, that their absence is more valuable to governments than their presence?

Many older public bathrooms in the UK were built on large sites and on what is, a century later, prime urban real estate in a country where land is at a premium. 'From a council's view,' says John Griggs, 'you can sell something for £4 or £5 million, or you can spend half a million [annually] on maintaining it.' The math's pretty easy there, given current austerity measures, the lack of value most people see in on-street, free facilities, and the reality that cafés and shops are serviceable make-dos. As it happens, one of Griggs's old schoolmates runs a business buying up old public toilets and turning them into restaurants.

In many North American cities where no old-school public toilets exist, it's the prospect of future maintenance costs that sinks any lust for construction. Finding capital is easy, one Toronto public servant told me, but ongoing maintenance costs, the finicky demands of users, and the difficulty of curbing vandalism, sex, and drug use is a pain in the arse municipalities aren't willing to sign on for. In this view, far from being seen as necessary parts of the urban commons, toilets have morphed into literal liabilities.

So is the answer *not* to build? But to still come up with a better solution than half-regulated networks of publicly accessible toilets where pee-ers pretend to be customers to earn their chance to go? Some municipalities pay businesses to display signage advertising their washrooms as no-questions-asked public spaces. One public bathroom on the Halifax waterfront is inside a privately owned building but open to the public. Placing it there and running it was a condition the developer had to meet for project approval. Ottawa's Joan Kuyek is on board with this kind of subtle coercion. She sat in her car in a parking lot one October afternoon and realized she was positively surrounded by toilets. Ever since Kuyek said this to me, I have moments of reflection, where I look around and silently count how many toilets there must be close by. It's quite a revelation, actually. Stand on a street corner and try it sometime. What if, Kuyek mused that day sitting in her car, businesses 'were given a small subsidy to put a sign outside to say "Public Toilet" and there was one down the street that said, "Public Toilet 50 Metres"?' Total game-changer.

Bichard, for her part, goes beyond the idea of subsidizing businesses to make up for municipal slacking off. She proposes a third way: an any-toilet, anywhere, anytime approach. Every building with a bathroom on the ground floor, including office buildings, should be accessible to anyone. No keys, no questions. Just access. She understands the instant opposition: security. But she's firmly against a fortress approach to public amenities. 'You can't keep treating populations like they're criminals,' she says. It's 'the death of the city.' (Tell that to Lake Station, Indiana, mayor Christopher Anderson who, in 2018, padlocked the doors to the city hall restrooms – men's *and* women's – because someone had repeatedly urinated in them, missing the toilet. Public and staff now have to get the padlock keys from the mayor's office. Some employees expressed disapproval to a reporter from the *Northwest Indiana Post-Tribune*, but none would speak on the record. 'I'm frankly surprised it's becoming this much an issue,' Anderson told the paper. But then, he's the one with the keys, isn't he?)

Just letting people use the bathroom is, in a sense, a far more out-there idea than enforcing code, or making laws that cities must provide on-street facilities for urban dwellers. Bichard's radical notion requires that we recast our idea of what's public and what's private. That we reinvent the place of bathrooms in the city commons.

In 2015, a Halifax Water employee was attending to a suspected fire hydrant leak when he was seen hopping behind a bank of mailboxes and urinating on a snowbank. A witness, a local home-owner, called the utility. Then he called the paper. In the story that followed, a representative for the city agreed with the offended homeowner that it's inappropriate for anyone to pee in public, saying that Halifax Water workers are expected to relieve themselves at municipal depots or publicly accessible bathrooms. But, he noted, employees often spend long hours in trucks on their shifts. The angry citizen pointed out in the story that there were a gas station and restaurant close by. The employee was disciplined, and, with no further word from the city, his motive – truculence or emergency – remains a mystery. But is the reason even relevant? After all, wasn't the water worker only doing the same thing as pet dogs?

We all know dogs have to eliminate waste like the rest of us. And the price we pay for having them as our pets is picking their poop off the sidewalk – and turning away when they pee all over trees, building corners, car tires, and the curb-side trash bags sanitation workers have to pick up. This is a practice unquestioned, a norm so entrenched, we barely notice the smells and sights. Laura Norén, whose essay about the bottle-peeing cabbies is called 'Only Dogs Are Free to Pee,' told me a story about living in the Chelsea neighbourhood of New York, a community of five-thousand-dollar-a-month studio apartments, art galleries, and lots and lots of dogs. 'These are people who would yell at someone if their coffee was not hot enough. At the top of their lungs. The entire neighbourhood smells like pee.'

What else can we do? Give up pet dogs in the city? Train them to hold it until some magical right place, right time that doesn't bombard city infrastructure with their urine? Perhaps all we can do is recognize the fact Norén points out in her essay: dogs have far greater urinary freedom than humans in the urban world. 'The amazing thing,' she says, 'is that more people don't just say, "Screw it. I am just going to pee on the street."'

6

THE INVISIBLE WOMAN

I can't even tell you how excited Neil is about his new outhouse. Neil and his wife, Carol, were a couple of years on the land – a pristine oceanfront slice of Nova Scotia's north shore with so-good-they-look-fake sunsets, a bunkie cottage, and nary a drip of running water – before they decided to design and build the privy. Before that, it was a roll of Charmin and a walk into the woods. The outhouse was a project for Neil and his soon-to-be son-in-law, Scott, a carpenter, restorer, and Canada Green Building Council–certified project manager. Scott knows his game. And the finished product, backed by Neil's unfettered enthusiasm, is a thing of beauty.

At least, until I tromp inside and pee all over the floor.

An outhouse is basically a protected hole in the ground for human excrement. Culturally speaking – even aesthetically speaking – there's not a whole lot of variation on the design. But Neil and Scott did a lot more than build a box platform on concrete and give it four walls and a door. This outhouse has upmarket khaki-coloured clapboard and plenty of natural light from a little crank window that looks out on spruce trees. The inside walls are pristine white; the door, carved wood with a brass lion knocker (a wedding gift to Neil and Carol in 1980). There's even a magazine rack and paperbacks. But Neil and Scott have only ever peed with penises, and without having consulted any vagina owners, their gorgeous little outhouse has one fatal flaw.

Men in Neil's outhouse stand and aim into the hole. Women sit. I may have to tell you, depending on the depth of your urethra knowledge, that men can point urine in any direction they fancy. Not women. Our urine exits the body at roughly forty-five degrees ahead of us. We gain a little tinkle-wiggle room by shifting forward or backward in any position, but whether we're sitting, standing, or crouching, pee exits our bodies roughly halfway to the horizon.

As I sat down to take that calamitous first pee in Neil's outhouse, resting on the comfortable wooden seat, magazine in hand, my urine hit the inside front wall of the seat's plywood box. It streamed down until it reached the spot where the box sits on top of the brand-new floor. I tipped up the bottom of my magazine and craned my neck to peek between my knees. Oh, I thought. Oh, dear. I watched, horrified – and quite unable to move enough to solve the problem – as my pee pooled into a puddle between my Birkenstocks. 'Men hit the back,' Neil told me later. 'Women hit the front.' Now it's fixed. Neil installed a piece of plastic that diverts women's urine into the hole.

Neither Neil nor Scott had built an outhouse before. But I don't blame this design flub on their inexperience. I blame it on the myth of the universal user. See, Neil and Scott were designing a space for men *and* for women (and for children, and for the elderly, and for a whole smattering of other users who might pop by for a cup of tea and need the can before they get back on the road). And while they probably didn't approach the job talking about designing for men alone, they also didn't approach it thinking enough about women.

Toilets are so run-of-the-mill and the need for them so commonplace (a human goes to the bathroom about 2,500 times a year), they somehow get lost in the folds of our consciousness. I get how it happens. We all have to go, and we all go through roughly the same range of activities – take down clothing, get into position, excrete, wash up – to do it. By this logic, it's no big deal to design a toilet; you just have to refer to your own experience. Except, as my creeping pee puddle shows, that experience is usually a man's, because the majority of architects, planners, designers, manufacturers (and outhouse builders, I'd wager, though I haven't been able to dig up stats on that) are men.

These professionals (and semi-professionals) aren't blind to the extraordinary needs of some – after all, wheelchair users fought and won to have specially outfitted stalls, and most bathrooms have changing tables for children in diapers – but the needs of women are hidden and nuanced. No one knows when a particular women is menstruating. There's no specific calculus for tallying up how much longer it takes women to negotiate the greater amount of clothing we must pull down or up to seat ourselves on a toilet. Neil and Scott weren't up to date on the position of my urethra. Clearly.

See, women have different needs, but not such visible or glaringly different needs that people are shaken into counting them. That's what makes toilets particularly a women's issue. Bathrooms aren't neutral spaces. And there is no universal user. Their design is loaded with pitfalls (not least of all the occasional puddle of urine) and their accessibility is loaded, too, with meaning. It has been this way for hundreds and hundreds of years.

Picture a woman. A dressmaker in 1900. Let's call her Ida. She lives in Camden Town, an inner-city district of London, in a crowded two-storey cottage with her parents and eight siblings. She commutes every day to her job at one of London's early department stores near Hyde Park, travelling with her workmates into the city core on the early workmen's train to save a few pennies. Thousands of women, and many more men, pass through Camden Town's centre, commuting to and from the district. Ida's train drops her off early. Eight o'clock. She kills time until her shift begins at nine. She finishes work at seven-thirty and takes the train home. At some point on either end of this commute, as anyone could well imagine, Ida might have to use the bathroom.

The Victorian fire for snazzy public conveniences was, when it came to facilities for women, at best a slow burn. By 1900, there were two public conveniences for women in Ida's Camden Town neighbourhood. That September, the local government embarked upon building a third.

Park Street at Camden High Street was a din of shouting newspaper sellers and tradesmen hawking wares from carts. The intersection was, and is still today, a willow tree of main roads. At the century's turn, the thoroughfare served a local population surpassing 200,000. Pedestrians hurried along and horse-drawn omnibuses made their way. Ida would have passed this teeming intersection on her way to and from work, or on trips to the shops. It's likely, too, that she would have seen the life-size wooden model on Park Street, set up by the local council to show the proposed location of the new women's convenience.

At the turn of the century, Camden Town's public works were the responsibility of the St. Pancras Vestry – elected officials who were in charge of streets, lighting, paving, and the like for the larger metropolitan borough. The vestry was also empowered – though not required – to provide conveniences where the need seemed obvious. And it was this council that was set upon by a band of residents and business owners who formed a delegation to oppose the new women's bathroom. 'There was this furious and very vocal reaction to it,' Barbara Penner told me. 'I just thought, how bizarre.'

Back in 1995, the renowned author of *Bathroom* was a masters student looking for a research topic that would allow her to explore the experience of women and the built environment. She found that in spades in Camden Town.

In fact, it was the Park Street women's lavatory brouhaha that first got Penner revved up about public bathrooms. She hasn't spared a glance back since. 'Gore Vidal, in the 1970s, describes public conveniences as hot buttons,' she tells me from her office in London. 'And I have consistently found that to be true.' When people argue over public bathrooms, Penner says, they're usually fighting about the right of certain social groups to occupy public space. 'Toilets,' she says, 'are a powerful way of signalling status, inclusion, and of maintaining social order and certain cultural values.'

All that in a toilet? All that in a toilet.

Dig into the Camden Town toilet debate, as Penner did in her indispensable 2001 essay 'A World of Unmentionable Suffering: Women's Public Conveniences in Victorian London' in the *Journal of Design History*, and it's clear it wasn't the Camden Town toilet per se that caused people's outrage so much as what the toilet represented. It doesn't seem as if this women's toilet could have been much different than its neighbourhood twin siblings. But women's bathrooms, at this time, would have held at best a shaky place in the public sphere. Providing bathrooms for on-the-go women meant acknowledging that women actually *were* on the go. But it was more than that. Because with public toilets, it's always more. (You've read this far – *you* know.) To allow for the necessity of women's public toilets was to allow that women had the right to move freely through the city. As more and more women worked outside the home, and as more and more women desired to simply *be* outside the home, the dearth of public bathrooms wasn't merely an inconvenience – it was a barrier to using the city. A barrier to being equal. And Western society in 1900 was happy to keep barriers to women's equality perfectly in place, thank you very much.

The Park Street public toilet wasn't just about women either. It was about working-class women. Installing a women's public convenience at a bustling intersection in the heart of a North London neighbourhood was providing for the hoi polloi. It would serve those like Ida, who lived in Camden Town and travelled to work in other parts of London, as well as the thousands of factory 'girls' who travelled into Camden Town for work. The wealthy (there were some in Camden Town – social surveyor Charles Booth's 1898 map of London poverty shows a number of Camden Town streets labelled 'Middle class' and 'Well-to-do') didn't travel like Ida did. Women of means moved around by private carriage, where they had relative seclusion – and the luxury of chamber pots when bodily urges struck.

Women without private carriages relied on public transit and, often, their own two feet. If they were caught short, they were well and truly caught short. Public conveniences, already rare for women, bore the prohibitive penny charge for every use. (Men, at this time, only paid to use water closets, not urinals. That women had to pay to urinate as well as defecate, wrote George Bernard Shaw, 'no man ever thought of until it was pointed out to him.') Shaw served as a St. Pancras vestryman from 1897 to 1903. And his 1909 essay, 'The Unmentionable Case for Women's Suffrage,' published in the magazine the *Englishwoman*, centres partly on the tribulations surrounding the Camden Town women's lavatory. His insights into women's privy privations don't come from that episode alone, though. During his tenure as a vestryman, Shaw received 'piteous anonymous letters' from women pleading with him to pressure the vestry to reduce the penny charge to a halfpenny, at least. London's large department stores (like the West End sort where our fictional

Ida earned her wage) increasingly had women's restrooms, but they didn't meet the demand of Ida and her ilk. They served customers only. Women with enough money to shop as a hobby.

Ida would have worn underclothes in the fashion of the day – left open at the crotch. This made squatting in alleys doable, but no less degrading. Sheer logic dictates that Ida would have found herself in need at least on occasion and without a respectable option for relieving herself. And she wouldn't have been alone. Shaw writes in his essay of the myriad complaints he received as vestryman about 'the condition of all the little byways and nooks in the borough which afforded any sort of momentary privacy.' When you gotta go, I guess, you gotta go.

Women's organizations and public health campaigners had called for increased provision for women near the end of the nineteenth century, to slim effect. It probably didn't help that the need seemed forever couched in hyperbole – Penner, in her essay, calls attention to health officer James Stevenson's 1879 report, which notes that not getting to the bathroom in a timely fashion worsens apoplexy (!) and causes disturbances of the heart. (In truth, bacterial infection is the most common side effect of holding urine, which, unfortunately for these Victorian women, causes the need to urinate even more frequently.) Vagueness was another pox afflicting the discussion of women's sanitation needs – Stevenson tiptoed around menstruation and pregnancy, hinting about 'conditions peculiar to the sex' when the 'requirements of nature are apt to be more urgent and more frequent.'

And women's public conveniences weren't exactly money-makers. Most of them didn't break even, and no surprise: those women who *could* afford a penny per pee avoided them because of their unmistakable tinge of immorality.

Women's conveniences reeked of supposed moral debasement on two counts. Since women's bodies have always been looked upon as vaguely and threateningly sexual and since the bathroom was a 'container' of bodily functions, to use Penner's term, the public bathroom was, by extension, faintly scandalous itself. Also, the potential mixing of classes inside bathrooms meant *ladies* would risk corruption by mere *women*. The Park Street lavatory debate, in this light, is too complex to paint as a mere fight for women's access. The push to beef up women's toilet provision was then, and is now, drowning in a slop of other issues – in this case, issues of social and economic class.

I'm selling public bathrooms in this book as a women's issue more than anything else. Women's needs, historically, have been hidden in society, uncounted by governments, and dismissed. It was no different in Camden Town. Consider: the St. Pancras Vestry, in 1900, included only two women, a Mrs. Phillimore and a Mrs. Miall Smith. Shaw, in his 1909 essay, argued that women's unique needs demand the presence of female representatives on public bodies. Alas – too bad, so sad – there were no women representatives for St. Pancras or anywhere else after the November elections of 1900, following a decree from the House of Lords booting women from borough governance altogether. The vestry did employ a female sanitation inspector, whose job it was to conduct quality checks on existing women's public bathrooms as well as the provision in worksites employing large numbers of women. The two vestrywomen had been the sole liaisons between the inspectress and the council; the vestrymen were, in a word, clueless. Shaw reported: 'The vestrywomen had always known what the inspectress was doing; but I, during my six years as a councillor, would never have discovered the fact of her existence but for the monthly salary list and the occasional necessity of replacing her when she left us.' The inspectress had reported what needed remedying, and Phillimore and Miall Smith had worked to find the will and the cash to get it done.

Once women could no longer sit on elected bodies after November 1900, the inspectress was left, in a sense, without a boss. She was employed, yes, and had a superior, certainly. But a report to the vestry by the female sanitation inspector was simply out of the question, since no respectable woman could talk about toilets in the company of men.

As Penner relays the events, in September, four men appeared before a meeting of the St. Pancras Vestry to voice their opposition to the Park Street lavatory. A representative of the omnibus operators named Mr. Tibbs argued that there was next to no need to accommodate women. He vouched that 90 percent of those passing by the intersection of Park Street and Camden High Street were local residents. The implication? They could – and should – find relief close by, at home. (Almost no working-class homes *had* much more than an outhouse or trough at this time, but that wasn't Mr. Tibbs's problem.) A Mr. White, representing residents of the area, opined that a women's convenience at Park Street and Camden High Street would degrade the neighbourhood. He was bolstered in his argument by Mr. H. Wakeley, who contended that property values would tumble on Park Street if the women's bathroom were allowed to proceed. None of these three men found it necessary to address the obvious logical inconsistency Penner points out: a gentlemen's convenience had existed at the same intersection for years, providing for men however close by or far off they lived, regardless of the state of their at-home provision, and completely without effect on the neighbourhood's moral character or the value of Park Street homes and businesses. In fact, seven men's conveniences dotting Camden Town had been built between 1890 and 1900 by the St. Pancras Vestry; it also provided temporary urinals when it had the urge. Conveniences for men were a no-brainer. A necessity. Tibbs, White, and Wakeley missed that particular irony.

Now, here's where things turn downright preposterous.

Mr. French, another omnibus representative, proclaimed that the proposed women's bathroom would impede traffic. It was too close to the street. His compelling evidence? The life-sized wooden model of the women's lavatory erected by the vestry had been hit by passing vehicles forty-five times on one day alone. Repeat: forty-five times. On one day.

Here's Shaw's retelling:

> Every omnibus on the Camden Town route, every trades-man's cart owned within a radius of two miles, and most of the rest of the passing vehicles, including private carriages driven to the spot on purpose, crashed into that obstruction with just violence enough to produce an accident without damage. The drivers who began the game were either tipped or under direct orders; but the joke soon caught on.

It's a farcical scene, no question. But it added up to more than mere mischief. As Barbara Penner writes, 'The men Shaw accuses were not mere pranksters involved in a spontaneous joke but, in many cases, respectable members of the community.' The fix was in for the Park Street lavatory, and the vestry chair was either oblivious or onside; he moved that the vestry find a better spot. Mrs. Miall Smith wasn't so gullible. She asked the vestry to investigate the claims of the four speakers. Shaw piped up that the chair's motion was a backhanded way of killing the project. Nevertheless, the motion passed.

Today, there is an underground public bathroom for women on Park Street at Camden High Street. The convenience rests right at the spot where the vestry's wooden model was bashed forty-five times on that day in 1900. At the end of 1905, London's Highways, Sewers and Public Works Committee had delivered a report recommending the building of a free women's convenience on that original site. The report was requested by the apparently indomitable Mrs. Miall Smith. London's vestry system had, by then, been replaced by borough councils. The council governing Camden Town agreed with the report and quietly began construction.

From the outside today, the Park Street bathroom is much like any typically inviting, attentive-to-detail UK public convenience of the Victorian era. It's made of wrought iron and white tile – and located, like many of its ilk, down a flight of stairs. It was exactly this breed of public bathroom that Susan Cunningham stood in front of in the city centre of Cardiff, Wales, in 1975.

Cunningham had come downtown on the bus to stroll the streets and do some shopping, bringing her toddler along for the trip. Everything was tickety-boo until her two-year-old announced that he needed to pee. *Now. Right now.* (Gee, have we heard this story before?) Cunningham faced a familiar dilemma – she was standing at the top of a flight of stairs with a push chair and a toddler, considering whether to start clunking the child, the stroller, her shopping, and everything else down the stairs, or to take a chance on a friendly-looking passerby.

This time in Cunningham's life was the hour of her toilet epiphany. She came to understand that if she wanted to be part of the city as a young mother, it meant a gauntlet run of stairs, too-tiny cubicles, and no changing tables for babies. She found herself giving real thought, for the first time, to people who use wheelchairs. 'This is the big thing about life,' Cunningham says. 'It's not until you get to certain stages in life, or have certain difficulties, that you become aware that the built environment isn't making life as pleasant and easy as it could be for you.'

This is also the story of Ida the dressmaker, of me going to the Halifax Common toilets in the early 2000s with my kids, and of Neil's outhouse, too. We have a hard time recognizing that things are a problem when they aren't a problem for us personally. Sometimes it's entirely innocent, like with Neil and Scott and the outhouse. Sometimes it's with clear malice, as with the cart-crashing street vendors and omnibus drivers of Camden Town. And sometimes? Sometimes it lies in between.

The Big Necessity's Rose George tells me about a story she wrote about the closure of public toilets in Leeds, where she lives. One day in 2012, George called one of the city's councillors.

'Okay,' she put it to the representative. 'Let's say I am sixty-five years old, and I am in Leeds at six o'clock on a weekday night, and I want to go to the toilet and you've closed down all the city-centre public toilets.'

'Well, you can just go into a bar.'

'I am sixty-five years old. I am not going to feel comfortable going into a bar. So what do I do?'

'Well, you can go to the bus station.'

'The bus station is three-quarters of a mile away. What if I have mobility issues?'

'Well, you can go to the train station.'

'That's half a mile away.' (I am half-waiting here for George to tell me that the councillor said she might as well 'go round the hedge,' as the Paddington Station manager once instructed Clara Greed.)

'There's just nothing,' George tells me, exasperated. 'Nothing available. And no kind of sense that there is anything missing either. That's what was more instructive. She didn't see anything wrong.'

That exchange screams meaning. It's the same feeling women must have faced in Camden Town, and all over the UK, in the early days of the public amenities movement, and the same thing

Cunningham felt at the top of those Cardiff bathroom stairs: this city is not for me.

Eyes opened, Susan Cunningham saw issues with toilets everywhere she went. She soon had another son. There were still few women's public bathrooms that accommodated nappy-changing, and even fewer men's bathrooms that did. As her boys got older, they wanted to go into the men's bathroom on their own. She worried for their safety, but there were no family bathrooms to speak of. That wasn't all. Women were still paying to use public toilets while men could use urinals for free. And, of course, there were the lineups for women's bathrooms. Lineups all the time. Lineups much like today.

'Women, from a very young age, are made to feel like it's the woman's fault. Women take longer. Her fault. And you still hear it! I have to keep my mouth shut. There are little girls asking, 'Mummy, why are we waiting?' 'Well, it's because women take longer.' Well, it's not. It's just that the planners, the architects, the local authorities, the people who license these places, are choosing not to be realistic, choosing not to give the space where it should be given.'

Cunningham was on the Isle of Wight a few years ago at a visitor centre when she noticed a group of children on a school field trip. All the children were using the bathroom before getting back on their bus. Two boys were standing to one side.

'Why are we waiting?' she heard one ask the other.

'We are waiting for the girls.'

'Why are we waiting for the girls?'

'They always take longer to go to the toilet.'

Cunningham's frustration shows as she recounts this tiny tale. 'They were about six, seven years old. And that's how it was. But that's not how it should be. You know?'

Forty years after her toilet revelation, Cunningham gestures to two jam-packed filing cabinets beside her desk. In them, together with a cupboard full of boxes in her loft, resides a written history of modern toilet activism in the UK. These are the files of All Mod Cons, the volunteer advocacy organization Cunningham started in March 1985 by sending a letter to the *South Wales Echo*. 'When I shuffle off this mortal coil, it's all going to go in a skip somewhere,' Cunningham says. But she does pull the files out from time to time to flip through, as she did before she sat down to chat with me. 'Looking through very briefly, I thought, crikey, I did work hard.'

Cunningham could rightly be called the mother of the modern toilet equity movement, though she resists the label: 'I think I have stuck with it a long time, with a lot of help from other people.' One of those people, her husband, Richard, mills around the main floor of their home in Cardiff as Cunningham shuffles through papers – survey results from the 1920s about the need for more women's bathrooms in major UK cities, a tourism survey from 1983 showing that Cardiff needed more and better public bathrooms. 'When we got to the year 2000,' Cunningham says, dropping her shoulders with a sigh, 'I thought: still queueing for loos.' And now? 'Still queueing for loos.'

You might call Cunningham an accidental activist, if it weren't for the fact that she threw so much of her life into toilets for so darn long. Early meetings of All Mod Cons were around her dining room table. It would be two or three young moms having cookies and tea, and talking about the dire state of public conveniences. It was about accessibility then – too few facilities for women, no accommodation for children, the strollers-and-stairs conundrum. Then came the continence folks, and the people with long-term disabilities. Word spread. Cunningham ramped up, researching so-called social misuse of bathrooms – like drug use and cruising, which were the excuses she found hurled at her by local governments for poor-quality or non-existent provision. She also started gathering data on menstruation, a side of the bathroom discussion often completely missing.

Soon Cunningham's role went beyond the media mock-up of a 'feisty housewife' (her words). She appeared as a speaker at conferences and as an advisor on government panels – most prominently, one that drew up the first British Standards for Sanitary Installations. The more people she connected with, the more toilet issues she learned about. The difficulties of caregivers trying to navigate the city with adults with mental illnesses or developmental delays; people who needed adult diaper-changing facilities; women with extremely heavy menstrual flows; a woman with two artificial hands who literally couldn't lock bathroom cubicle doors. 'That's an extreme example,' Cunningham concedes, 'but what about people with arthritis?' (In fact, design researcher Joanne Bichard has done lots of research on this front, and Cunningham is right on the mark – not being able to work fiddly cubicle locks or flush with the often hidden or weensie little mechanisms is a major problem for the elderly. My grandmother, at ninety-two, could get around town just fine, and loved to be out and about, but her fingers were bent and arthritic – she had a hard time with anything requiring dexterity, including pulling bills from her wallet, inserting bus tickets into the automated wicket, and, I bet, pressing those tiny toilet flushers. I don't know for sure, though: she was too proud to ask me to come in and help.) As her activism grew, and the more Cunningham understood the problems with bathrooms, the more she perceived that bathrooms signal a social hierarchy based on whose needs are met and whose are not. But, for her, it always came back to women: 'It's a fact, historically, that the provision of public toilets for men has always been better than that for women.'

Cunningham is an optimist. She doesn't see the lack of women's provision as outright misogyny, but as a bigger-picture oversight. A failure to provide for communities. Local governments in the UK, as we've learned, have zero legislative responsibility to build and maintain public toilets. The British standards for public conveniences are merely strong advice, not law; the most commonly legislated minimum ratio in the UK of 1:1, in the context of women's actual, on-the-ground needs, isn't enough. It's patently not potty parity. Building proper public bathrooms is a complex business, and it can be a costly one. But what helps women generally, helps everyone. Cunningham calls it 'enlightened self-interest.'

There's one more issue that's central to the issue of potty parity. But menstruation, I'm afraid, rarely gets discussed. By sheer volume alone, however – nearly a quarter of all women of child-bearing age are menstruating at any one time – it's one of the critical pieces of the public toilet discussion. You can't control blood the same way you control urine. You can't hold it in. 'If people are sort of flooding,' Clara Greed told me (as if I needed to be reminded – who of the ovary owners among us hasn't had to tie a sweater around her waist to hide a period catastrophe?), 'they need to change their tampon or sanitary pad.'

Even when we're not on our periods, women have different bathroom needs than men. And when we are menstruating, women have *patently* different bathroom needs. We pee even more frequently, and so need more public bathrooms we can access around cities. We take longer in stalls, because changing tampons, pads, and menstrual cups takes extra time, which contributes to lineups; and we need proper disposal for sanitary products in stalls, since flushing these products can cause plumbing problems.

It bears mentioning that pregnancy also presents unique bathroom needs and challenges that should rightfully be accommodated (being knocked up means not only increased frequency and urgency of urination; any nine-months'-pregnant woman who's tried to lower herself onto a toilet seat understands the usefulness of a grab bar). But menstruation stands out because of its commonness – from about age twelve, most women will menstruate for three to five days, once a month, for about forty years. I'd be remiss here not to mention, again, that many trans men have periods, too. No matter how you slice it, that's a lot of bleeding.

Call menstruation the third sanitary function. Urine, shit, and blood are our excretory trifecta. And menstruation has been almost perfectly unknowable to the (mostly) cisgender men designing and installing bathrooms in public buildings and public spaces. It is the last bathroom taboo.

Rose George says women have learned to think we are 'dirty for having periods' and that we've been socialized to not talk about supposed 'icky bodily functions.' She tells me a story of being in rural India, researching *The Big Necessity*. She was staying at a cheap guest house and, as one is apt to, she needed sanitary pads. She walked to the spot where a drugstore kiosk sat in the street and asked one of the handful of men behind the counter for the pads. She felt inexplicably ashamed. The man put them in a brown paper bag and she paid. 'I had this sort of ancestral mortification about it,' she says. 'It's ridiculous.'

Well, it is, really.

As a journalist and author who researches excreta and how societies deal with it, George isn't bashful about bodies, nor about any of the things that come out of them. So, why? Why shy away when it came to publicly dealing with her period? Why did a Heathrow Airport guard searching her bag at security take her package of menstrual pads and hide them under her other belongings? Why do I never rinse out my menstrual cup in the sink at a public bathroom?

The briefest look at menstrual product advertising over the past one hundred years spells an answer. Periods are a secret. Periods represent shackles (while commercial menstrual products equal freedom). The ideal period is when no one knows you're on your period and, moreover, you barely know yourself. 'We are just bombarded on all sides,' George says, 'from advertising that is telling us to hide it, to be fragrant, to be discreet.'

And discreet we are. Or at least euphemistic. George specifically calls out the mysterious blue liquid used to illustrate absorbency in TV and print ads for menstrual products. A notable departure is UK pad company Bodyform, which launched a series of online ads in late 2017 using red liquid as a stand-in for menstrual blood and boasting the slogan 'Periods are normal. Showing them should be too.' It's great, but I'll hold off on calling this a revolution in clear-headedness until the rest of the pad companies follow suit. 'It works the same way in general with toilets,' George says. 'When have you ever seen a toilet roll advertised for what it actually does? Instead, it's about puppies and rainbows.' Where even euphemism fails is in some developing nations, where periods are so mired in stigma as to be practically unutterable. A 2016 UN report suggests that one in ten girls in sub-Saharan Africa is absent from school during menstruation, due to lack of facilities. Clara Greed says this is easily as serious a development issue as education and employment, but it's rarely given the same weight.

'If you think sanitation is neglected,' says George (it is; don't forget those numbers off the top: 2.3 billion without basic sanitation, 892 million who defecate in the open, 842,000 poor-hygiene–related deaths a year), 'menstruation is far worse. You've just got stigma, upon stigma, upon stigma, upon taboo, upon unspeakability.' If women here, there, and everywhere have trouble openly acknowledging our periods, how are bathroom designers supposed to accommodate them? 'I think it's a women's problem,' George says. 'I think it's women who don't talk about it.'

Maybe.

Susan Cunningham remembers being 'howled down' at a meeting of feminists in Cardiff for talking about the need for public toilets for women. She doesn't know why, exactly. But I have an idea. Women tread a fine line when it comes to talking about equality by way of special treatment for issues of the body. Women are always at risk of being presented as biological beings, as hostages of our bodies. It hearkens to a past mired in weaker-sex myths. And it hearkens to a present where women are still often valued – and judged – for our bodies before our brains, where the unique work of our bodies – like having babies – can still damage our careers. No wonder women are so touchy about body politics. When Barbara Penner started talking about toilets as a feminist issue, she got walloped. 'Women didn't want to be tied to biology in this really immediate and really kind of pungent way,' she recalls.

In 2005, Penner published an essay in the *Journal of International Women's Studies* discussing the response to her public bathroom research. Various groups, she tells us, were skeptical that bathrooms were a legitimate line of inquiry – feminist theorists among them. Talking about the special needs of the female body – and that's exactly what we talk about when we talk about lineups and poor design – 'threatens to reassert a chain of connections,' Penner wrote, 'which feminists have worked hard for decades to destabilize.'

Rose George's take? Pfft…whatever.

George says women can't avoid the fact that we are subject to hormonal change. That we are biological creatures. She loves the story of the Great Britain women's field hockey team, who send their period dates to their coach so he can tailor their training. 'Because it's normal,' she says. 'But it's not.'

'It's normal, but it's not' may be the most banally truthful statement we can make about menstruation. It's both normal, and it needs extra attention. Especially when it comes to public bathrooms. That paradox really comes out in reactions to women speaking publicly about menstruation – we are alternately set upon, like Cunningham and Penner were, or lauded. British tennis player Heather Watson broke the period taboo at the 2015 Australian Open, saying her poor performance was a result of dizziness and nausea caused by her period. Social media was less than kind. And worse to female elite athletes who nodded approvingly at Watson's 'bravery.' When George wrote a piece in the *Guardian* about Watson's remarks, it garnered the most comments of anything she'd ever written for the paper. And, tellingly, the most comments deleted for offensiveness.

Women's – and society's – relationship with menstruation may change over time, but what doesn't change is menstruation itself and the need to deal with it. In Halifax, where I live, we have never had more than a (small!) handful of on-street public conveniences. In other cities where public toilets had once flourished, their removal is epidemic. 'We call them conveniences,' says George, 'but they are necessities.' And more for women than anyone else. So why are we not out in the streets, demanding more? Women are very good at coping,' says Cunningham. 'Managing, getting on with things.'

The great women's public convenience debate aside, there was one question Barbara Penner was never able to answer about the unrelieved women of Camden Town: how did they manage?

How did Ida, my fictional dressmaker in 1900, get to work and back home without provision? What exactly did she do when she had to go? The women of Camden Town were, in any real sense, unknowable to Penner. And unknowable to those in whose midst they lived – from the powerless female sanitation inspector to George Bernard Shaw. Sure, Shaw was an advocate for women, but Penner argues he also revelled in the titillating exoticism of the female body. The working-class women of turn-of-the-century Camden Town were, Penner writes in her 2005 essay, 'only ever glimpsed in sideway glances, through the rhetoric of the male councillors, medical health officers, sanitary engineers, journalists, and Shaw himself.'

Penner researched the surviving documents of the Ladies' Sanitary Association, an early and vocal proponent of provision for women, including in Camden Town. But she found women's difficulties in navigating the city described in vague terms: public health, sanitation, hygiene. 'None of these sources give a sense of the quality of women's experience – how did they manage it?' Penner wonders.

We don't know.

7

KICK AT THE CAN

Fall 2014: Mission Theoretical.

If I'm a tourist in downtown Toronto (which I am), and I have to pee (which I don't, but, like, give it a little time…), can I find one of the city's three fabulous, sparkling automated public toilets? I'm walking in the right direction, I'm sure of that – west from Yonge Street along the waterfront. And I'm certain the bathroom is there, because I Google-Street-Viewed it so I'll know what it looks like when I see it. But after a solid fifteen minutes of plodding, I realize it's fortunate indeed that my mission today is only notional. Because if I actually had to pee, I'd be up shit creek.

Toronto is Canada's largest city. Near 44 million tourists a year hit the region's streets, people who certainly need places to relieve themselves. The bathroom I'm hunting is on Queens Quay, a main thoroughfare that runs parallel to Lake Ontario. I could map it on my smartphone while I'm walking, sure, but I want to first see what would happen if I didn't have that particular luxury.

Toronto's Harbourfront district is far from a no man's land. I'm walking toward the CN Tower and Rogers Centre, where the Blue Jays play home games. I pass the Toronto Island Ferry Terminal, a plaque commemorating Babe Ruth's first professional home run, plenty of public art, benches, and expert landscaping. What I don't pass is a bathroom. Or a sign for a bathroom. I stumble upon a Waterfront Business Improvement Area map, encouraging me to eat, shop, play, live, and stay here. But apparently not go to the bathroom, because that amenity is missing from the checklist. Finally I break down.

'Siri,' I beg the butt end of my smartphone, 'where's the closest public toilet?'

Siri, ever-cheerful, bursts my balloon. 'I didn't find any public toilets.'

On I walk.

There are bathrooms here, of course. They're everywhere. In the snack bars and cafés, and the art gallery facing the waterfront. These are washrooms hidden and assumed – toilets that exist as part of the secret city. If you find them, you find them. If you don't, you don't. If you have nerve, confidence, and you look kempt, you get in. If you think you don't belong, if you're too shy to ask, or if you're dishevelled, you're out of luck. I fall into the former category. The potty privileged. But relying on social advantage isn't part of today's mission. Onward.

Finally, I spot it, set back from the corner of Queens Quay and Rees Street. The building is generous for a single-user bathroom – about four metres by four metres, on a concrete pad with an outside bench. The exterior is graffiti-free, a tasteful combo of light grey and aqua green, matching the city's bus shelters. It costs a quarter to get in. (I know this and I've excitedly packed several in my jeans.) But my change stays pocketed today. Not because this toilet hunt is purely academic. But because this toilet is closed.

I stand across the street from the Harbourfront toilet, taking in the cacophony of construction and the makeshift fencing surrounding my potential potty paradise. The bathroom is a temporary casualty of a $150-million street renovation to make Queens Quay more pedestrian-friendly and welcoming for tourists. (Oh, the irony here today.) Past the shards of debris, on the bathroom's sliding steel door, I see a redundant paper-and-Sharpie sign: 'OUT OF ORDER.' (Though I have to wonder: is it, in addition to being cloistered inside a temporary three-metre fence, *also* broken?)

Walking to get to a toilet – and often finding it inaccessible – is something Toronto's homeless population of over five thousand does many times a day, every single day. Doug Johnson Hatlem knows plenty of people who fester on the streets in urine- and feces-soaked clothes because they lack easy access to bathrooms. Hatlem grew up in California. I call him in Chicago, where he's working as a full-time dad. But for eight years, he was a street pastor with Sanctuary Toronto, a Christian charity and outreach centre located in a former church and gospel hall just minutes from the downtown nexus of Yonge and Bloor Streets. 'Everything is considered church,' says Hatlem about Sanctuary. 'But they do a lot more than Sunday stuff.' A big part is getting to know Toronto's street community.

Hatlem says business owners and people designing public spaces aren't merely failing to think of good ways to accommodate street populations, they are actively trying to keep the homeless out. Charging for toilets is not the underlying issue here, Hatlem says. Instead, it's the sense that toilets are only for some, and not others. The pattern goes like this: people on the street feel separated – often *are* separated – from the rest of society. Because of that, they are frequently unwelcome in the publicly accessible toilets in shopping malls, fast-food outlets, and coffee chains. That puts them at risk of soiling themselves. And when that happens, Hatlem says, 'you stink. And you are feeling even more outcast.' The cycle restarts.

Epidemiologist David Waltner-Toews writes, in *The Origin of Feces*, that in eighteenth- and nineteenth-century Europe, bodily odours were connected with 'lower' classes. Cleanliness, as you probably guessed, was a ticket to godliness, so dousing oneself in perfumes was a way of flaunting one's economic prosperity and one's righteousness. Waltner-Toews argues that this concept has stuck, along with the ridiculous myth that poor people can tolerate substandard sanitation and the resulting smells better than those with more money and 'more sensitive dispositions.' Doug Johnson Hatlem points out another, related myth: that homeless people only go into bathrooms to mess them up. He understands the desire to keep publicly accessible bathrooms clean. He used to work in a restaurant with a washroom that was open to the public. But he categorically opposes barring the homeless. 'If people talk kindly, and act kindly and respectfully, and welcoming, and do the best they can in those particular circumstances, it works.' Treat people respectfully, Hatlem says, and people will show respect back.

In 2000, pastor Greg Paul was in charge of renovating the washrooms at Sanctuary. The ones being gutted were the original 1916 bathrooms – 'really grungy, typical old church-basement stuff,' Paul, the centre's co-founder, says. A significant part of the Sanctuary community is 'pretty volatile,' he tells me. Some face serious mental health issues, long-term addictions, and post-traumatic stress disorder. Pre-renovation, community members routinely smashed the mirrors, wrote on the walls, and trashed the bathrooms. No surprise, then, that the initial plan for the bathroom renovation was to 'bullet-proof everything.' Then staff had a brainwave. Steel and cinder block reflected the insides of jails, hospitals, and locked wards, places where many Sanctuary members had faced significant past trauma. 'We wanted a space where people would feel honoured, honourable, and respected,'

Paul says. So they went out and bought two giant mirrors. Nice mirrors, two square metres. They ordered custom cabinets, toilet enclosures made out of wood, and regular porcelain toilets. Polished won out over penitentiary.

Up to a thousand people use the Sanctuary space every week. Post-renovation, it was years before there was any graffiti. When they pulled out the toilet enclosures in 2013 for some repair work, there were two bits of scrubbed-off graffiti in the men's. Nothing in the women's. The thirteen-year-old mirrors were still intact on the walls.

Chris Bateman is waiting for me across the street from the Harbourfront automated public toilet. 'I didn't realize!' he says, palms up to the pell-mell construction activity. Bateman is a professorial-looking freelance journalist wearing a brown corduroy blazer, a pocket square, and argyle socks. He's agreed to meet to enlighten me on the middlebrow history of Toronto's public bathrooms. We dart away from the mess and noise to find a bench as I apologize for being late. Bateman understands. 'I think the problem is that unless you're from here, they seem hidden,' he says.

Bateman grew up just outside London, England. He moved to Toronto in 2011 and he's probably as close as Toronto is going to get to a public toilet historian. It was all a fluke – Bateman was at the archives looking at nineteenth-century photos for another story he was researching when he noticed, in one of the black-and-white shots, an ornate iron railing to…nowhere. It turned out to be Toronto's first public bathroom, built in 1885 on Toronto Street, opposite what was then the central post office. The bathroom was an underground, male-only amenity, with four urinals and three stalls, and an attendant who shined shoes and kept order. The entrance down to this groundbreaking public work was, inexplicably, smack dab in the middle of the busy street.

As Bateman discovered in his research, there had been plenty of calls for public conveniences in Toronto toward the end of the nineteenth century and into the twentieth. It seemed like everyone wanted them. Thing is, no one wanted them anywhere near their houses, or their businesses, or their places of worship. The same supplicant-obstructionist political conundrum bubbled up when the city put in its second public bathroom (again, for men only) twenty years later, at the corner of Queen and Spadina. That one, too, ended up right in the middle of the busy thoroughfare. 'The answer,' Bateman discovered, 'was to put the entrance an equal distance from everybody's buildings.' (Though how *lasting* an answer is another question – the Queen and Spadina bathroom was pulled out of service after several years because it was so damn hazardous.) The pattern played itself out with Toronto public toilets into the 1920s: we need these facilities, but we want to pretend they're not there. 'The sense I got from it,' says Bateman, 'was that it was a sanitation issue.'

Kind of.

The terms *dirty* and *sanitary* convey more than the spectrum of cleanliness when it comes to bathrooms. Ask yourself: how do you actually feel about public bathrooms? For most people, they are considered the epitome of filth. And that's regardless of how dirty or clean they actually are. We don't revile toilets merely because they are places where we deposit our worst waste either. After all, if we really felt so horrified about bathrooms themselves, how would we ever stand to have them inside our homes? The 'sanitation' issues Bateman saw in his research of Toronto's early public toilets may have been couched in terms of actual dirt – fear of odour, particularly, was a driving objection to that first Toronto Street bathroom – but more likely, the objections really stemmed from a fear of *social* dirtiness. That is, the idea that only those in certain circumstances – the working class and the homeless – need public bathrooms. (That's for men, anyway. Women, as we saw with the hubbub over the Park Street Lavatory in Camden Town, weren't supposed to need bathrooms at all, ever.) Equating public toilets with the poor makes both the people and the facilities things to be avoided, derided, and looked down upon. 'When you think of "dignified,"' says Abigail Brown, a sanitation activist and sociologist, 'you think of an upper-class individual who fits into the mores of the social economy. So, if you are not able to provide that for yourself, then you are automatically put into a box – unhygienic.'

Toronto stands as a decent case study in the rise and fall of public toilet provision. *Popular* would be too strong a word for bathrooms in the context of the history of Toronto, which by 1900 had a population of 200,000. There were never more than fifteen or twenty on-street (including both above-ground and subterranean) bathrooms in the city at one time, Chris Bateman guesses, and they were always floating in a municipal provision murk. Needed but not wanted. They had the potential to be great equalizers, but they showed a mean streak of social stratification. Toronto closed its stand-alone public bathrooms one by one over the mid- to late-twentieth century as they broke down, became difficult to maintain, and – often precisely as a result of being broken and dirty – went mostly unused. Another tactic used by Toronto officials in the face of not-in-my-backyard toilet upset was to shunt them away in parks. It was a devious cycle of self-fulfillment – moral objections pushed toilets into the shadows, the shadows made them less safe and less visited, and that bolstered their bad reputation.

Alongside the ongoing ill feelings about public toilets, Toronto passed a seemingly progressive bylaw in 1921 requiring every new gas station to provide a public bathroom. Gas stations would bloom like algae in Toronto and across the country through the twentieth century, as they would in most major North American cities. Fuel stations reached a peak in Canada of more than twenty thousand by 1989. That's a lot of bathrooms. But that original bathroom-adding legislation would have an unforeseen lasting impact – it would become an early step in Toronto, and other municipalities all over North America, washing its hands of providing bathrooms for citizens.

The rise of the gas station rest stop raised a slew of still-lingering questions about who's responsible for providing hygiene and toilet provision for the mobile and for the most vulnerable. Today, in addition to the three automated toilets, Toronto has a year-round permanent 9 a.m. to 10 p.m. bathroom facility at Nathan Phillips Square, outside city hall. (In it: three toilets and three urinals for men, and three toilets for women, making it 2:1 in favour of men. Sad trumpet.) There are also a number of park bathrooms – though most close at night, and most for the entire winter. Officials rarely hear calls for more, I was told by Elyse Parker, of the City of Toronto's public realm section, when I spoke to her in 2014. 'As the city densifies, there are more and more opportunities to use bathrooms in restaurants, in stores, in cafés,' she said. 'Starbucks has kind of become the new public toilet.'

But Starbucks hasn't been an option for everyone. Ask Philadelphia's Rashon Nelson, who was told in April 2018 by a Starbucks manager that he couldn't use the restroom because he wasn't a paying customer. He and business partner Donte Robinson – both African-American – were then arrested as they waited at a table for a meeting with a third man about a real-estate transaction. Nelson and Robinson allege racial profiling, and their story, to me, is a perfect illustration of what Robert Brubaker worries about with supposedly publicly accessible bathrooms versus public bathrooms. In the wake of the incident, Starbucks declared its bathrooms open to anyone, so long as the customers – paying or merely hanging out – weren't disruptive. Though this take-all-pee-ers approach has long been the informal policy at Tim Hortons and it certainly didn't help the angry pooper in British Columbia. So how much will it aid street-outreach clients stuck walking the streets in smelly, wet trousers?

This is where Toronto's automated public toilets could make a real impact. And this is why I've gone on this Harbourfront toilet mission – the Hunt for the Queens Quay Loo. In 2007, Toronto signed an agreement with Astral Media to install and maintain twenty of these toilets across the city over twenty years: all of them available twenty-four-seven, year-round. The bathrooms come prefabricated at 250,000 bucks a pop; installation costs can near-match that amount. The units require water and sewer connections, and hydro. They are heated in winter and air-conditioned in summer. 'It's really like putting in a small house,' Parker said. Once she put it that way, the half-million-dollar cost per unit made more sense. Though in this scheme – as with most such agreements between media companies and municipalities (think New York, for one) – none of this cost would be borne by the city. It would be Astral's role to buy the bathrooms, install the bathrooms, and maintain a three-visit-a-day cleaning schedule over the twenty years of the contract. In exchange, the media conglomerate would own the exclusive right to sell advertising on Toronto transit shelters and information columns.

In Parker's estimation, the total profit was to be one billion dollars over twenty years, with a minimum of $429 million coming directly to the city through revenue sharing, and likely more. But the toilets have proven challenging to site – ostensibly because of their size, but I'm going to go ahead and suggest there's some classic toilet NIMBYism happening, too. So where does that leave Toronto? Three APTS have been installed and a fourth is planned – so far, so good – but eleven of the original twenty toilets have been 'cashed out' to provide the funds to bail a private bike-share program out of debt.

What now?

Deep breath… Toronto, in 2011, signed a ten-year loan guarantee for $3.9 million to help Bixi, a private company, set up a for-profit bike-sharing system in the city. The bikes were popular. Well, in any case, popular enough that the city wanted to keep them around, but not so popular that the company could meet its loan payments. Meanwhile, a clause in the Astral street furniture contract allowed the city to force the media conglomerate to pay a sum – in this case five million bucks – for the privilege of *not* building all of the promised toilets. So the city conveniently canned eleven of the toilets, Astral paid the city five million clams, and that money was siphoned off to cover the bike-share debt, plus transition costs for the city to take over the bikes, which were clearly more desirable than toilets. (I guess if Torontonians are caught short, they can hire a bike to get them to the next closest public toilet, huh?) If you're counting toilets (out of twenty, three installed, one in progress, eleven dead) – that leaves five. A handful of toilets that city spokesperson Cheryl San Juan, when I followed up with her, put in the 'to be determined' category.

With a cool billion in potential revenue in the original deal, you might rightly assume that a quarter-per-poo charge is a drop in the bucket. Toronto street furniture manager Carly Hinks calls the fee 'nominal.' The first two APTs had been getting used about ten thousand times a year, Hinks told me in an email in 2014. It would be less now, almost certainly, since all three existing APTs are closed December 1 through April 1. (What? Have Toronto's toilet honchos been taking cues from Halifax and St. John's?) Even assuming ten thousand flushes a year, at twenty-five cents per use, that's $2,500 – less than half the estimated annual cleaning and maintenance costs. So why charge at all?

The real value of those quarters, Elyse Parker told me, is that they deter vandalism. 'For whatever reason,' she said, 'it makes a difference. It's just one of those human things.' Chris Bateman, though, likens toilet fees to 'a bouncer on a front door.' And he doesn't mean it in a good way. 'It's more of a way of telling people that maybe certain standards are expected in this washroom, or only a certain kind of person is allowed to use it.'

'They think it gives you a cleaner toilet,' says Gail Ramster (the creator, as you may remember, of the Great British Public Toilet Map). 'But it doesn't. The places that charge in London are no cleaner.' Her assessment of the failure of pay-to-pee is anecdotal but ample. Ramster has been researching public toilets for more than five years. She and her colleagues at the Royal College of Art have interviewed more than a hundred public toilet users and overseers. Her conclusion: you can't force respect. When I chat with Ramster as she sits in a glassed-in meeting room at the Helen Hamlyn Centre for Design, I am reminded of the messy women's bathrooms at the mall I frequented as a child. By the prevailing logic, as pay toilets, they should have been pristine, but former manager Bob Pasquet had recalled they were not.

Paying for toilet access falls under the broad scope of an urban planning principle called 'crime prevention through environmental design.' Other such design measures related to public bathrooms include stainless-steel or resin toilets (which can't be broken), having no toilet seats (which can be removed or smashed), installing metal mirrors (smashing, natch), having no mirrors (to prevent gay sex; we'll get into that in a jiffy), prohibiting paper towels (which can be set on fire, though equally flammable toilet paper gets to stay), removing in-stall shelves (which apparently aid drug users), and installing uv black lights (whose bluish gloom, I'm told, prevents people from seeing their veins to inject drugs – must be hell for lipstick application, too). These fixes make it tricky to vandalize a bathroom. They also make it tricky to actually use one. This goes beyond whininess over the discomfort of cold steel rims and preferring paper towels to air dryers. In the quest to keep people from doing what they aren't supposed to in bathrooms, Ramster argues, some crime prevention design is stopping people from doing what they actually need to: using the toilet.

Ramster's co-researcher Jo-Anne Bichard says crime-prevention design measures are especially problematic when they're applied indiscriminately. That is, when all users are punished because of the relative few using toilets for drugs, sex, or vandalism. Her example: mirrors. In men's bathrooms, mirrors are used for cruising – men make eye contact with strangers as a prelude to sex. But when mirrors in a given men's bathroom are removed to curb cruising, they are often also taken from the women's – 'even though,' says Bichard, 'we don't look in the mirrors and run off and have sex together.' What women do instead is use mirrors to check our appearance. 'In our society,' Bichard says, 'we have to check how we look, because we are so judged by the way we look.' No one, least of all me, thinks this is the way the world *should* work. But there's no denying that's the way the world *does* work – women's success in many arenas depends unfairly on looking put together. Women use bathroom mirrors to check how we look. But with no mirrors, we can't.

Another casualty of blanket anti-vandalism measures? Those in-stall shelves. The ledges, usually sitting near the back of toilet cisterns, are designed to hold the gear people need to lay out when they change a colostomy bag. Or to support a purse, a water bottle, a hot coffee, or a shopping bag. Crime-prevention design principles, though, say the shelves pull double duty as a place to line up, and snort, cocaine. So it's goodbye to the shelves and good luck to anyone with a colostomy. Or, you know, any other small item you can't hold while you pee but would prefer not to lay down on a bathroom floor. And how about those uv black lights? They're one of Bichard's favourite design bungles. She smiles cheekily as she tells me why – it turns out that some people, as one of her research colleagues discovered, find them erotic: 'So, whilst the people who wanted to inject drugs moved out, the people who wanted to have sex moved in.'

Ramster and Bichard believe crime-prevention design measures should be location-specific, and argue that if a public bathroom is more welcoming – and, as a result, better-used by so-called legitimate users – then there's less opportunity for anti-social behaviour. ('Although, having sex isn't really anti-social, is it?' Bichard jokes.) There are examples of toilets that have been *de*-vandalism-proofed – spots where community groups have taken over council-closed bathrooms, cleaned them, and spruced them up with flowers and artwork – and they've actually become more vandalism-proof in the process. This is how I think about the Herald and Greeley Square bathrooms – they've been made less likely to be wrecked by virtue of installing objects that are easily wrecked, like glass flower vases. There are shades of Greg Paul's Sanctuary toilet renovation in this argument, too, found in that conscious choice to install eminently smashable two-metre-square mirrors. The idea is deceptively simple: by not assuming the worst of people, you end up getting people's best. This reasoning applies broadly. 'If you go in and there's toilet paper all over the floor,' Ramster says to me, 'then if you drop toilet paper on the floor you are less likely to pick it up. Right?'

I've been trying to answer a question here: does the quarter charge to use the Harbourfront automated public toilet keep it cleaner? But let's forget that query for a moment and consider something perhaps more important: is a quarter affordable for the people who must need these toilets most? Sure, Doug Johnson Hatlem says. People on the street can come up with a quarter. But most won't waste it on going to the bathroom. 'If they are trying to scrape together eight bucks to buy a bottle of wine, for instance,' says Hatlem, 'they are not going to use one of those quarters to go to the bathroom inside.' And it's not just one quarter either. A middle-aged man typically defecates once a day and urinates six to eight times. Using the automated public toilet religiously could cost a homeless person sixty-seven dollars a month. In recognition of that potential hardship, the City of Toronto instituted a program in 2010 that allows its outreach workers to give away free tokens for the automated public bathrooms so people don't need to spend money.

But when I asked Elyse Parker about the program, she admitted there hadn't been a lot of uptake – likely, she suspected, because of the locations of the toilets. The second APT was built seven kilometres east of the one at Harbourfront, on Lakeshore Boulevard in Toronto's Beach neighbourhood: which placed both toilets in areas Parker suggested are not particularly well-travelled by the homeless. The third one was built almost five kilometres west, also on Lakeshore Boulevard. Hatlem says there are definitely street people around Harbourfront (Bateman and I were approached by a man panhandling while we chatted outside the Queens Quay APT), but in all his time in Toronto (he left in 2013) he'd never heard of the token program. Neither had Karen Eacott, an outreach worker with Covenant House Toronto, Canada's largest youth shelter, nor had two other people working with homeless youths and adults in Toronto I contacted – though city spokesperson Cheryl San Juan confirms that the tokens are still provided to vulnerable populations through city social services.

So if the homeless and poor aren't using the automated public toilets, and have difficulty accessing bathrooms in cafés, stores, and restaurants, where, exactly, are they going when they need to go? We saw the answer in San Francisco: anywhere they must. 'We have certainly seen lots of places where there is defecation in downtown Toronto,' says Hatlem. Eacott has frequently seen it, too. 'You can kind of guess whether it's human or not,' she told me. Toronto's defecation problem is something of an open secret, as it is in San Francisco and many other major cities. While there's a burgeoning international awareness of the problem of on-street defecation in the global south and in developing nations, in the developed world we mostly either don't see it or pretend it's not happening. Abigail Brown says people should quit kidding themselves. 'We have it,' she says bluntly. 'In cities everywhere.'

But less, perhaps, in some places than others.

The Portland Loo is a vandalism-proof, twenty-four-hour flush-toilet enclosure. An anti-tech fix for on-street public bathrooms. The Loos are simple, oval-shaped rooms with a toilet. They're spacious enough to fit strollers, wheelchairs, and even bikes. In contrast to the high-tech entrances, timers, and air-conditioning systems at work in conventional APTs like those in Toronto and New York, Portland Loos are naturally lit and ventilated and completely off-grid. They also happen to be an example of the successful use of crime prevention through environmental design – louvred sides allow people on the outside to see that there's someone inside while maintaining privacy, and exterior handwashing sinks get people right out after they use them. The loos pepper Portland, Oregon, and are popping up in cities like San Diego, Victoria, and Seattle, where Portland Loos have started to replace that disastrous fleet of APTs the city yanked out and sold on eBay. They are well-used – though that's anecdotal. Bryan Aptekar, a program specialist with Portland Parks and Recreation, says the city doesn't have a way to count restroom users; it's not something Portland has ever felt the need to track. But here's a hint: the Portland Rescue Mission runs a publicly accessible 24/7 bathroom with flush counters – they log 400 flushes a day, about 146,000 a year. That tells you something. Toronto has five times the population of Portland, but the Harbourfront toilet sees just 6 percent of the estimated visits of the Rescue Mission bathroom. The Portland Loo has overcome that deeply entrenched sense we have of public toilets being synonymous with filth, that they're bathrooms of last resort, or that they're primarily for the poor and homeless.

How?

First, the City of Portland treated the bathrooms as a civic responsibility, not a means of leveraging advertising revenue. Second, the loos have nothing whatsoever to do with homelessness. This is more progressive than it sounds at first blush. Carol McCreary helped design the Portland Loo. She's a co-founder of Public Hygiene Lets Us Stay Human (the brilliantly acronymed PHLUSH), a Portland-based toilet-advocacy group. PHLUSH is well-mobilized, wide-reaching, and volunteer-run. It's got its finger on the flusher of toilet matters, from environmental concerns to emergency measures. But PHLUSH's signature issue – and one it consults on across the US and into Canada – is urban public toilet design. The two questions McCreary gets most often: 'How do we provide for street-involved people?' and 'How are we going to build all these toilets with all these homeless people around here?"

Neither question is the right one, says PHLUSH member Abigail Brown, because on-street public toilets are for everyone.

'If you have a small child, they don't have as much bladder control as an adult,' she says. 'If you have a child in diapers, or caregivers of people who don't have as much mobility or ability to control their bladder. Individuals who suffer from Crohn's disease. Tourists. People who are exercising, out running, elderly individuals. Everyone.' So PHLUSH's answer to the conundrum of toilets and homelessness has been to cheerfully ignore it. 'We decided that we would not be discussing homelessness at all,' says McCreary from her kitchen table. 'That we would never build a toilet for the homeless. Whatever we were going to promote would be for everybody.' Free to use. Tax-supported. (Almost the total opposite of the Toronto and New York APTs.)

The loo was the brainchild of former Portland city commissioner Randy Leonard, who was brave enough not only to address public bathrooms and demand solutions, but who imagined them as a civic boon rather than a civic drain. In his wild vision, the city would design and fabricate a public toilet so durable, easy to maintain, and relatively inexpensive that Portland would sell them to other cities to subsidize the cost of maintaining its own fleet. 'Frankly,' says Bryan Aptekar, 'that has played out.' Aptekar says it took some time, but council as a whole adopted the aspirational vision of the Portland Loo, and over the years it has installed twelve of them across the city. And, in turn, Portland residents have come over to the loo side, too. In Oregon and other US states, residents are sometimes asked to vote on bond measures – pools of proposed funding for capital investments or critical repairs that don't fit into already-approved budgets. How it works is the city issues a bond, just like in the investment industry, and voters promise to repay the money over the lifetime of that bond. It's a way for the city to responsibly go into debt to cover urgent needs. In 2014, Portlanders voted yes on a bond measure allowing Parks and Recreation to spend an additional

$68 million, in part to replace faltering and high-cost bricks-and-mortar public bathrooms with Portland Loos. 'We are wholeheartedly in,' Aptekar says. And the 'we' he's talking about is Portland – not PHLUSH, not a few social justice–minded city councillors, but the city as a whole.

There are droves of bathrooms in the restaurants, malls, and bookstores dotting North America's urban cores. But there's perhaps no potentially greater friend to pee-ers in need than the well-maintained, spacious, unisex bathrooms at Starbucks. In 2014, Canada had the highest per-capita rate of Starbucks in the world, with forty cafés for every million residents. The US came second, with thirty-six cafés per million people. (My back-of-the-napkin calculations tell me the US has since edged us, with almost forty-three Starbucks per million in 2017.) So: Starbucks? Ubiquitous.

The question: are they really public?

They're technically free. But technically not. There's no cost, but the cost isn't exactly nothing. And this applies even in light of the new Starbucks policy that *anyone* can use their cans. Because there are still people there – customers and employees alike – who are monitoring these spaces to assess user legitimacy. People can still be refused access. And remember the bigger picture: the new Starbucks model of bathroom provision is on the far end of openness. Most other café chains won't venture even that distance toward acceptance. See, bathrooms aren't perfectly public when there are 'Customers Only' signs, or when access is enforced by way of locked doors that require employee-doled-out codes, remote-access locks, or keys attached to giant shame sticks kept behind the cash. Bathrooms don't feel public when access is controlled through the demeaning stares of staff and other customers. All this speaks to the deeply ingrained understanding of the public bathroom as a privilege that must be paid for. That is, something that customers deserve and others do not.

What *is* a customer, anyway? Does someone need to buy fries to be a McDonald's customer? Anyone test-driving a car would certainly be considered the customer of that car dealership. People use washrooms in shopping malls and hotel lobbies without necessarily spending or staying. In many retail and commercial environments, customers are defined not only as those who buy, but as those who appear as if they *could* buy. Given this, it's really no surprise that Elyse Parker told me she doesn't hear much about the need for more on-street toilet access in Toronto. Most people either have money to buy some nominal item, or they have the *appearance* of money, which gains them easy access. The poor and the homeless? They just don't have a voice.

Worth mentioning here is the nuance of privilege. Covenant House's Karen Eacott says lack of bathroom access is a problem that rarely comes up in her work. Street youth, she says, usually don't sleep rough (that is, literally on the street). More often, they are in shelters, squatting in abandoned buildings, or couch surfing. They're highly resourceful, share info, and work together. They know which internet cafés and fast-food joints will let them use the washroom or stay for extended periods – 'a lot of places are good,' says Eacott. 'They will let people sit there for hours, overnight.' The profile of a street youth, then, is markedly different from that of a long-time street drinker, who is often a lone man. 'It's probably easier for people who are younger to panhandle,' she adds. 'So it may be easier to come up with two dollars to be able to buy something to become a customer to use the washroom.' This kind of unspoken inequity is the reason PHLUSH's McCreary is adamant that a public bathroom should never be defined by the question of what makes a customer. A public toilet, she says, is defined always and only by who funds it. 'It's about more than just having clean cities for the people who are well-off,' says Abigail Brown. 'Just like we need air to breathe, we need water to drink, and we need places to relieve ourselves. I mean, it's about human dignity.'

I've got a plane to catch. It's a virtue of Toronto that one of its airports is accessible by foot, and I walk there whenever I visit the city. But I'm not going to make this miniature commute if I don't stop for a pee on the way. The theoretical need I set out with this morning, on my mission to find the Harbourfront toilet, has by this point become actual. Chris Bateman walks with me as far west as he can before we say our goodbyes. Then he strolls northward home, where he's got a bathroom waiting for him any time he needs it. 'When you actually step back and think about public washrooms in depth – which I don't think a lot of people do – it's a missing piece in looking after people,' Bateman says. 'They are so basic, too. That's what really blows me away. It's not like they would only benefit some people, or one portion of society, or one part of a community. Really it's for everybody. Literally.'

We shake hands and I nip gratefully into, you guessed it… Starbucks. I'm glad, as I have been many times before, that I'm lucky enough to be able to just waltz in and use the facilities. Nothing stops me. No locks, no codes, no keys. No growly employees glare at me. In fact, I get a smile. No scornful customers judge me as I scamper in. I go. I wash my hands with warm water and soap. And I open the locked door. And then? I get in line and I buy a green-tea latte, stamping my invisible pee pass. Why spend the six bucks? Because something unshakable and mysterious tells me it's the right thing to do, even if I know it really isn't.

8

STALL TACTICS

The men aren't old. But they aren't young anymore either. Sixty-five, let's say. They share a speedy gait to the door of the mall bathroom, chatting, oblivious. The first turns the knob. Locked. Only then does he notice, right above his hand, the numbered keypad. And above that, a sign telling him access is for customers only. It takes him a few seconds to read it. The men share a look.

This bathroom is in a mall food court, about three metres from the end of a coffee shop. The first man walks to the counter and says a few words to the guy wiping up with a cloth. It's Sunday morning and quiet. Otherwise, he'd probably have to wait in line, maybe buy something, maybe not. The barista, who says later that he engages in this mundane exchange throughout every shift, nods understandingly and tells him the five digits. The man returns and lifts his hand to punch in the code. Then, finger locked in the air in front of the number pad, he pauses. He rummages in a pocket and gets out his glasses. He puts them on, leans his torso back to bring the keypad into focus, and fingers in the code with staggering jabs. He tries the knob again. He's in. Let's say the whole thing has taken about two minutes.

'That might be too long for me,' Alexandra Murdock says, as we watch.

'I don't know if this is too much info,' she continues, 'but with a bowel movement, the longer you hold it, the more forceful it is. I have jeans on, I have the buckle, the button, the zipper.' Murdock also has Crohn's, an inflammatory bowel disease that, along with its intestine-mate, colitis, affects one out of every 200 Americans and one of every 150 Canadians – among the highest rates in the world. 'You'd never know by looking at me,' she says. It's true – at thirty-two, Murdock is slight and sprightly. Her diagnosis took nine months, when she was twenty-three. First it looked like the flu, then they thought a parasite. She couldn't consume much more than cans of Boost or even walk up a flight of stairs. She was in and out of the hospital. But she wasn't just sick. She was a time bomb: 'I could go to the bathroom twenty times a day.'

Her Crohn's is stabilized now, through medication and a careful watch over her diet. But the nervousness that goes along with Crohn's hasn't ever left Murdock. Every time she leaves the house, she knows where the closest toilet is. And not just vaguely: 'If we go to a restaurant, before I sit down, I know where the bathroom is.' She has to. If she has a Crohn's flare-up, 'it's not in ten minutes. It's not whenever I find it. It's now.' After Murdock and I watch the men go through the motions of gaining access to the mall bathroom, we walk over to the barista. I ask: does he just give out the bathroom code to anyone? 'Yep,' he says. 'It's five-four-three-two-one.' Murdock asks why they're locked. 'It's not up to us,' he says. 'It's the mall. They lock them just to be difficult, I guess.'

That little keypad lock is a barrier designed for, well, for *what*? What's the point? Those two men found a way in with relative ease. Another time, when I went to the same mall, months later, someone had taped the code – still five-four-three-two-one – above the keypad. But even granted that grace by minor social disobedience, poking in the numbers is still an unnecessary slow-down. And for people who can't deal with delays – when it's not ten minutes or ten seconds, it's *now* – bathrooms like this are more than merely annoying. They are a huge problem. The uncertainty around them leaves people anxious and 'panic-stricken,' Murdock says. Feeling like they don't belong.

Imagine a matching barrier – seemingly small and mostly unthought-of – that might affect someone with a physical disability. A broken automated door opener that would prevent someone who uses crutches from getting into a bathroom without another person holding the door, for example. Or an unusually high floor transition at the entrance to a bathroom that would be an issue for someone using a wheelchair. Would obstacles like that get any more recognition from the general public? Would those barriers get cleared up any faster? I think they would. People with physical disabilities – the ones others can see – have fought hard to have their accessibility needs met. And they've mostly won.

The 1950s through the 1980s were decades of awareness-raising around the challenges of people using wheelchairs, those who use crutches, and those with hearing and vision loss. State and local governments started setting out accessibility standards in the US in 1961. But it wasn't until 1990, under George Bush Sr., that the Americans with Disabilities Act became federal law, barring discrimination against anyone in schools, workplaces, or other public spaces because of a disability. The ADA is sweeping legislation that has made accessibility the expectation in new and extensively renovated buildings. (Though, as I write this, it's under attack, after House Republicans passed legislation in

February 2018 effectively removing incentives for businesses to comply quickly with ADA rules.) Similar federal legislation doesn't exist in Canada or the UK, but both countries have reasonable, quilted-together coverage protecting people with disabilities and enabling access to public spaces and transportation.

Accessibility laws started coming into effect in the mid-twentieth century. Of course, people were having a hard time moving around – because of loss of limbs from accidents, from developed diseases like polio, or from congenital disabilities they'd had since birth – long before that. American president Franklin Delano Roosevelt was in a wheelchair for the duration of his time in the White House, from 1933 until his death in 1945, but it wasn't common knowledge. Before mid-century, people with congenital physical ailments were generally viewed as flawed – those who developed them later in life, worthy of pity. Disabled military members returning from the First and Second World Wars were thanked for their service but, ultimately, found that society that didn't have a great deal of room for them, despite their skills and sacrifices. Public transportation wasn't accessible, nor were most workplaces or schools. These veterans were politely shoved to the side.

But during the late 1950s and 1960s, the push for disabled rights grew alongside the civil rights movement – and gained dubious help from the Vietnam War, which saw yet another generation of military men returning from the front, many needing rehabilitation and demanding reintegration. No groups with special needs, from transgender people to those with invisible disabilities like Crohn's and colitis, have ever been as cohesive and loud as the physical disability rights community. That lobby became and continues to be, a quarter century after the passing of the ADA, a powerful political force. We see the impact of it in pretty much every public building, and public bathroom, we enter. But that doesn't mean everything is perfect when you're in a wheelchair.

Emily Duffett has routes that she sticks to. And, she says, 'I know the places to avoid.' Duffett was born with spina bifida. She used crutches and walkers early on, but by age nine she had lost the use of her legs and started using a wheelchair. When I first meet her, she's cheerful, twenty-six, a social worker, and the chair of Canada's National Educational Association of Disabled Students. She laughs easily, but when it comes to accessibility, she's no mincer of words. Most public bathrooms, she says, are only 'someone's definition of accessible.' She has to admit, and she surprises me when she does, that she can't think of a single time she's waited for an accessible stall in a multi-stall bathroom. But everything isn't always sunshine and lollipops. She points out that what she needs in a bathroom, access-wise, may be different from the next person with a physical disability. Because of that, Duffett says standards must be broad and updated frequently if they are going to be worth anything. She cites a friend with a wider wheelchair than her own, which measures about three-quarters of a metre across. The woman was at a hotel and needed to use the lobby bathroom. To do so, she had to climb out of her chair, crawl into the toilet stall, fold up the chair, and drag it in. There is access, I guess, and there is access.

Duffett and I are touring the accessible washrooms at a large regional children's hospital in eastern Canada where she spent a lot of time as a kid. The first we come across is probably four by four metres – a bathroom bigger than Duffett's bedroom. There's a spiffy movable support bar beside the toilet that slides up and down depending on the height the user needs, which is good for people with balance problems or those who use walkers, she explains. The soap, toilet-paper dispenser, and mirror seem to be at good heights. But Duffett quickly reverses her smile. The door lock is on the high side. I'm not tall, but the paper-towel dispenser is level with my neck, making it ridiculously high. And the coat hooks are another twenty centimetres above the top of my head. The sink is fine, but Duffett points out a concern not easily addressed. Manual-chair users like her need lower sinks; power-chair users need higher sinks. The question is: go with one or split the difference?

The next bathroom we scope out leaves her little room to get in, but she manages. The support bars, door lock, and soap dispenser are good, but the light switch is at my chin. Duffett stretches up but has to give it a few hits before it fires and we can see our surroundings. Some bathrooms, she says, use sensor lights – which sounds like a solution until she tells me they usually fail to register when she wheels in because she is so low in her chair. Behind bathroom door number three, there's barely enough space for Duffett to manoeuvre, and she can do so only after shifting a garbage pail. The soap dispenser is almost unreachable, the mirror isn't angled, and its bottom edge is fifteen centimetres above her. In it, she can only see the ceiling and the top of the wall behind her.

I put it to Duffett: what's an ideal bathroom? 'I don't know if there's an answer,' she says. I recall what she told me about sink height. What works for one user may not for another. And, as with the sensor lights, it's common in design to inadvertently create problems as you fix them. Automated bathroom doors are another good example – they remove the need for people to push and hold doors while manoeuvring a wheelchair through, but when the circuit shorts out, or the unit gets turned off because people are playing with it, users are left with an extra-heavy, almost unopenable door. 'Even a good [bathroom] can be bad, if you know what I mean,' Duffett says. I do.

And there's this problem: even the best building codes grow stale with age as equipment evolves and as the idea of who, as a matter of rote, should be included in our thinking about inclusivity changes. Just think about Duffett's friend crawling on the bathroom floor into the stall, yanking her folded-up chair behind her. That was an accessible stall. Or, at least, at one time it must have been good enough: it never would have passed the building inspection for that hotel lobby otherwise. As part of her work, Duffett does accessibility consulting – helping organizations boost physical access, and access by way of policy, procedure, and attitude. She says the problem is not so much that the general public doesn't see the need for changes to buildings to suit people who have difficulties with mobility. It's that they think too narrowly about the solutions. Meanwhile, accessibility for other users – the invisibly disabled – isn't even on the table.

A 2014 DirecTV ad posits this concept: there are two Rob Lowes. One is the chiselled, articulate movie star, who has DirecTV. The other is Painfully Awkward Rob Lowe, who sports high-waisted Dockers, a fanny pack, and a middle-part, and still subscribes to DirecTV's competitor, traditional cable. Suave Rob Lowe has an upscale house and makes blender drinks while his many pals mingle and watch boxing on DirecTV. Painfully Awkward Rob Lowe shares the decor taste of *The Golden Girls* and loiters alone by his picture window, waiting for the cable installer, who, he frets nervously, may be 'a girl.' At the end of the commercial, Painfully Awkward Lowe stands in front of a urinal beside two other men in a public bathroom. 'Fact,' he says over his shoulder to the camera. 'I can't go with other people in the room.'

The message is, of course, to choose to be the right Rob Lowe, the one with friends and money, not the awkward loner who can't pee in public bathrooms. The commercial, one in a series that compares DirecTV Rob Lowe with other, inferior, cable-subscribing Rob Lowes (like Crazy-Hairy Rob Lowe and Peaked in High School Rob Lowe) is – I'll say it – funny. The spots are far from politically correct, and that's the point. I get it. You probably get it. My neighbour's teenaged boys definitely get it. Even Steven Soifer gets it.

Soifer is a Memphis-based clinical social worker and CEO of the International Paruresis Association. He started the IPA two decades ago to heighten awareness of paruresis and advocate for people with the condition, more commonly known as shy bladder syndrome. Paruresis is the difficulty or impossibility of using a toilet or urinal anywhere there are other people around, or where the sufferer believes there are other people around. It's classified as a social anxiety disorder in the American Psychiatric Association's *Diagnostic and Statistical Manual of Mental Disorders*. Soifer is also the man who, on Twitter, called out DirecTV and Rob Lowe, calling the Painfully Awkward character 'demeaning.' Lowe hit back, tweeting that his bladder was 'gregarious' and that people needed to lighten up.

Soifer doesn't like the ads – but, he says, the IPA got mileage out of it. He appeared on the American talk show *The Doctors* and was interviewed for stories in newspapers and magazines. The public response wasn't exactly sympathetic – even some shy-bladder sufferers criticized Soifer's blasting of Lowe – but as far as awareness of the condition goes, it was mission accomplished. Previously clueless people learned that shy bladder syndrome existed, and others suddenly understood it was more than just the quirk of a few weirdos. Doctors are years away from understanding the mechanisms of paruresis, but they know it's both psychological and physiological. Keeping tabs on numbers is 'nebulous' – that's Soifer's word. 'Anyone I talk to can tell me a toilet story where they were not able to go. But for some people, that sticks, and shapes the rest of their life.' The condition is believed to affect 7 percent of the population – some 22 million people in the US alone.

Perhaps ironically, given the Rob Lowe kerfuffle, having a shy bladder is widely thought to be caused by bullying. That's what Soifer hears most from the people he treats for the condition, and that's how it happened to him. He says paruresis has never really made a significant impact on any of his major decisions – except one date, which ended at a tiny Brooklyn flat. 'The bathroom is here,' he says, gesturing with his hand, 'and the bed is here. That was the end of the date.' Others make all their decisions based on the condition. He's known hundreds of people to change jobs or pass up a promotion because their existing workplace bathroom situation is safe, and the new situation involves travel or office-mates. Two examples he cites: a journalist who works as a newspaper deliverer, a medical student who can't finish a residency. He knows of a woman who can only pee late at night in her backyard. He knows people who are functionally agoraphobic, who might go to the store and shop for thirty minutes, but who have to be close enough to get to the bathroom at home. 'Anecdotally,' he says, 'I have heard of one prisoner who committed suicide because of the problem.'

How do public bathrooms come into all this? After all, it's not like public bathrooms will ever be the same as the ones we have at home. We can never rid them of other people in them. Their reason for being is their capacity to be shared. The answer comes squarely on the design front. Changing small details in the ways public bathrooms are put together – relatively easy, inexpensive fixes – can benefit many and have little to no effect on the experiences of others.

For men, bladder shyness is primarily about visual privacy. So let's picture the common scene in a men's bathroom. A line of close-together, low-bowl urinals with no privacy dividers, or a dreaded trough urinal, in clear sight of the line of people waiting for stalls. That's a nightmare for the pee-shy. For women, it's mostly about auditory privacy. That's where traditional, open-bottomed cubicles – so-called 'surveillance' stalls – become a non-starter. Proximity comes into the condition, too: the closer people are, the harder it is to go. A 1976 study showed that men who urinated close to other men in public bathrooms took longer to start peeing, and peed for a shorter duration than when they were farther from strangers. That study looked at sixty random men, not ones affected by paruresis, so the phenomenon may well affect anyone. 'Design is such a big part,' Soifer says. 'It doesn't solve the problem, but I would say 90 percent of people, if they were in a soundproof bathroom where there weren't people waiting, they could go.'

Oy, but there's the rub. Soundproofing we can manage. But how can we stop people from waiting to use bathrooms? There's only one solution for that. More bathrooms.

When people have Crohn's or colitis, their bathroom needs are episodic and urgent. Episodic, because they don't have problems, or even the same problems, all the time. And urgent, because, as Alexandra Murdock made clear that day we met for the first time – and hung out at the mall watching old men gain access to that code-locked bathroom – a small delay in getting to a toilet can make the difference between a normal day and shitting your pants. Help for people with most diseases of the bowel comes not in the form of design modifications, but by way of fast and easy access to bathrooms. Everywhere. This fix requires no changes to bathroom configuration, no additional installations, no changes to building code, no investment of money or infra-structure. Yet, as we've seen with so many other bathroom woes, easy fixes – social fixes – are often the most difficult. Folks with urgent, invisible bathroom needs in one sense require the highest level of accommodation, because it boils down to this: Please, stranger, let me use your bathroom right now, because I really, really need it.

Jennie David remembers shopping with her mom. David is a doctoral student in clinical psychology at Philadelphia's Drexel University. She was diagnosed with Crohn's at twelve. Early on in her process of settling into the idea of living with Crohn's, she was at a Walmart, using the store's accessible bathroom stall. When she opened the door to come out, a woman was waiting, clearly unimpressed that David had opted – needlessly, to her eyes – for the accessible stall. 'The way she looked at me, it was like, "What a vile young girl, so disrespectful." And then I see her at other places in the store. You know, she has no authority over me, I know nothing about her. But she stared me down. And some people have the guts to say things to your face.' David deals with questions around the medical legitimacy of her condition all the time. See, David looks healthy, and acts healthy, if there is such a thing, yet she has great health challenges and extraordinary bathroom needs. 'If I had no hair, it would be different,' she says. 'What? Am I supposed to lift up my shirt to show them?'

David sits on a floral duvet on her white metal bed. Her posture shows she spent her youth as an accomplished dancer. Beneath the top of her loose grey T-shirt, a port-a-cath pokes out. An IV tube snakes from it to a bag on a pole. She is chatting with me during the lengthy stretch of time she needs to be home to treat the chronic dehydration that's caused by her Crohn's – two litres of sodium chloride solution, three times a week. The infusion takes four hours, which works just fine, since we have a lot to chat about, and David is no longer the twelve-year-old who used to sit by the phone waiting for her gastroenterologist to call to tell her she'd been misdiagnosed. She is happy to share.

At nineteen, David had an ostomy. She had the lower portion of her colon and, in her case, her rectum, removed. Her feces now collects in a bag attached to a hip-level stoma, which is the protruding end of her lower intestine. 'I couldn't wait,' she says, talking about the surgery, and that's both urgency and excitement in her recollection. She had gotten progressively sicker over the years after her diagnosis, and progressively less able to control her bowels. For about six weeks before her surgery, she tells me, she was in adult diapers, with a commode within arm's reach at all times. That's why there's freedom with an ostomy. 'There is not that rushing. You go where you walk.' But an ostomy is not without its challenges. David's stoma swells a little at high altitudes, so she has had small leaks on airplanes. And so any time she flies, she must check, clean, and sometimes change her bag. To do that, she has to lay out the kit she carries with her in counterless airplane bathrooms, where a small mess can quickly become a bigger one. David carries cards – one that says she has Crohn's and another that says she has an ostomy – that give her legal access to employee-only bathrooms in states where that legislation exists. She is likewise entitled to use accessible bathrooms, because the Americans with Disabilities Act covers her – at least for now; let's see what changes the new Republican legislation might bring. But even though she knows she's allowed by law to use the bigger stalls, she isn't always at ease doing so. Shades of Walmart. 'If there is a line in the bathroom, technically I can go up and say, "Look, I have a chronic illness. I need to use the bathroom."' But she almost always waits. 'It's interesting that, for someone who is an advocate, and who is open about it, I still find myself doing things I don't need to be doing.'

Is the solution here legislative, or it is social? Is it that people with invisible disabilities must strong-arm the unwitting and the unwilling, or that society needs to be more understanding of, and educated about, diverse needs? Crohn's and Colitis Canada, for its part, is betting on a more-flies-with-honey-than-vinegar approach. GoHere is a decal program encouraging businesses to post stickers on their doors if they've got open bathrooms; in exchange, the shops or restaurants get free advertising on the Crohn's and Colitis website. The GoHere campaign is reminiscent of rainbow flag decals on stores that want to show support for the LGBTQ2IA community. The sticker changes nothing about the business's merchandise or services, but it changes customers' feelings and, in theory, their willingness to support a given business.

Alexandra Murdock says simple directional signage would be a huge factor in easing her Crohn's-related bathroom tribulations. You'll rarely see a directional sign for a close-by bathroom on a downtown street, she points out, while it's not uncommon to see signs on roadsides for casinos, museums, and other attractions that are kilometres away. Of course, for the fix of more and better signs to work, there must be public bathrooms in the first place. It's a particular irony that in the UK, enforcement of the 1995 Disability Discrimination Act has been blamed for the closure of many of the Victorian-era subterranean toilets. Some local authorities installed elevators; many said they couldn't afford to retrofit for wheelchairs and shuttered or sold off the bathrooms instead.

But, really, aren't we all pretty much one step away from life events that could – and will – change our relationship to public bathrooms? Decreased mobility is something almost all of us will face in our lives, whether by way of an accident, aging, or heredity. Most of us will confront these challenges in ourselves, and in those we care for. And we'll suddenly find that the bathroom-stall status quo no longer works for us either.

The University of Illinois's Kathryn Anthony has written books about the effect of design on people's lives and has testified before US Congress about potty parity for women. But she also has a deep personal connection to the issues of accessibility in public bathrooms. Her late husband had cancer for seven and a half years. He died at forty-six. At the very end, he was in a wheelchair. 'Only one week,' Anthony says, 'but we went places. He was well enough to get out and about. He didn't look good, but we lived in a teeny-tiny place and he needed to get out and get fresh air.' Where Anthony connects to the accessibility issue isn't so much on the details of access – sink height and support-bar placement, for example – but on issues of gender neutrality and the need for bathrooms big enough for caregivers to accompany people who need assistance. Her husband was too weak to open bathroom doors, too drained by illness to easily move himself. But they had a difficult time, on their outings, finding bathrooms where Anthony could accompany him, and she often had to wait outside, fingers crossed that everything would be okay.

Around that same time, in 1998, a nine-year-old boy, Matthew Cecchi, was murdered in a beachfront public bathroom in Oceanside, California, where he was attending a family reunion. A man had gone in, killed the boy, and walked out, all while Cecchi's aunt waited for him outside the men's room. Digesting the horror of this story, which happened near Anthony's San Diego home, and reflecting on her own experience with her husband, galvanized her views of gender-free accessible bathrooms. For her, they solve a few different problems – they give vulnerable people privacy; they allow caregivers to assist the people they are caring for in the bathroom, regardless of their gender; and they boost parity, because women can use these spaces just as readily as men. 'It's a family issue,' Anthony says. 'I think that's the way it really needs to be seen.'

Accessibility is a family issue in a simpler, more material way, too. Many of the barriers affecting people using canes, walkers, and wheelchairs also affect parents and caregivers pushing strollers. That's why Anthony calls 'healthy parent, healthy children, using wheels' a 'mobility impairment.' While accessible bathroom standards mean people with disabilities can (ideally) reach toilets, urinals, and sinks, parents with small children have to lift kids onto toilets, hang on to them so they don't fall in, and hoist them up to sinks. Stepstools help, but finding them is hit-and-miss. Writing about this now, I am smacked with flashbacks of all that hauling and holding I did as a parent – so many near-plunges into toilets; so many times my kids had their shirt fronts soaked by the wet sink counters I balanced them against, supporting their bums with one knee as I held them under the armpits to help them reach the faucet. Child-sized toilets exist (I mean, you can just order one off Amazon), and children themselves are ubiquitous in many public buildings, but it's practically unheard of to see mini-toilets outside of preschool bathrooms. Small-sized urinals? Occasionally. Plainly, Anthony says, 'people with disabilities have been far more successful than parents with children in having this issue heard.'

Where parents have been heard, the result is often that they are lumped into the accessible stall. More often than not, that stall is where you'll find the baby-changing station in small public bathrooms, and sometimes in larger ones, too. And parents aren't the only ones elbowing in on accessible space. Call me a bad person, but I take up the accessible stall when I'm travelling with a suitcase. Anthony, on this front, sympathizes: 'So many travel facilities do not have access for us when we are carrying suitcases and luggage. You can barely close the door and the suit-case sometimes touches the edge of the toilet.' She closes her eyes and shudders with her shoulders. 'We are mobility-impaired because of what we are carrying.'

When the accessible and family toilet is its own separate, gender-free room, transgender and gender-nonconforming users can access it to avoid having their gender scrutinized in the men's or women's rooms. Parents of physically able kids on the autism spectrum, too, often find it helpful to send their children into the separate bathroom, where the youngsters can have more control over the commotion and sounds that can cause them upset in multi-stall spaces.

There are two ways to look at all this space-sharing. On one hand, it's recognizing diverse needs and making use of flexible space to accommodate people. But it's also potentially taking space from people who need it. After all, parents with children, people with luggage, transgender folks, and those on the autism spectrum can all make do in other stalls. People with wheel-chairs and those who use walkers cannot. If anyone else is using their stall, they have to wait. Anthony likes that space for people with disabilities can be used by others who decide they need it. But, she says, it's not without risk: 'That's the chance someone takes when they use one of those stalls. They keep out someone who genuinely needs it – that is, who is mobility impaired, or is in a wheelchair.' I find it interesting that most people will use an accessible stall when there is a queue, but the same people, I'd wager, wouldn't take up an accessible parking spot at the mall or the grocery store if the lot were full. But then, cops don't give out fines in bathrooms. (At least, not for that particular transgression.)

The population with special bathroom needs is often passed off as inconsequential – by the numbers, small. There are some convenient factors that allow this myth to stay put in people's minds. Primary among them is that going to the bathroom is a private act, even in a public space. And there's this: visibly undetectable conditions are just that – undetectable. Half the people in a multi-stall bathroom with you at any given time could be, say, struggling with hypersensitivity to the deafening hand dryers and auto-flush toilets, emptying ostomy bags, holding one kid on the toilet while another is crawling from under the stall, changing an adult diaper, or trying to drown out the world with headphones so she can pee. You don't have a clue what's happening inside those stalls. Finally, tragically, there's this, from Jennie David: when the issues become too big, when finding a bathroom in public just becomes too much of a gamble, people stop going out. It's then that they go from being merely unseen to being invisible. The problem isn't solved. It's shelved.

'Something is wrong here,' Kathryn Anthony says. 'I wish we weren't all as self-centred as we are. But some of these issues, until they hit you personally, you are not aware, and you are not as bothered by them.' Steven Soifer, of the IPA, once came up with a figure – a quarter of the population, he says, maybe a third. 'If you figure out the entire spectrum of people who have different needs at different times. Seven percent have paruresis. Another 7 percent are incontinent. You're already up to 14. You throw in menstruating women, parents with kids, people with ostomies…' He stops there, trails off. Too many to count.

9

WAR AND PEES

Gabriel Enxuga was in a bathroom stall in a bar. The men's room. And not alone. A transgender friend was having a binding emergency – the Ace bandage he used to flatten his breasts was coming loose. Enxuga was helping him rebind when he heard pounding against the door. He froze. 'Faggots!' *BAM*. 'Faggots!' *BAM*. 'Faggots in the men's room!' *BAM*. *BAM*. *BAM*. Enxuga panicked. He didn't know, once the stall door opened, whether he would get beaten up for being transgender (which he is) or beaten up for being bisexual (which he also is). He felt trapped and scared. 'At that point in my life, I had not yet begun medically transitioning and I often didn't get read as male. So I didn't know if they would open the door and think I was a lesbian, a trans person, or a gay man.' Enxuga takes in an audible breath. 'None of those possibilities seemed like good options.' Enxuga and his friend knew they couldn't stay in the stall forever, but they didn't want to take their chances with whomever was on the other side of the door. So they stayed put. After a time, which Enxuga remembers being both short and long, security arrived and the pair were kicked out.

The self-appointed toilet police are everywhere. In men's rooms, they're on the lookout for errant glances in mirrors, too many pairs of feet, or toes under stall partitions tapping out invitations for sex – anything that suggests the presence or mere possibility of homosexual encounter. That Enxuga was in the right bathroom for his gender, as a trans man, and that there was nothing sexual about his being in the stall that night with his friend, was entirely beside the point. Social restroom regulation is all about keeping these spaces as straight as possible. And it makes male bathrooms one of the last and brawniest strongholds of heterosexual supremacy.

In women's bathrooms, policing plays out differently, and it tells of a different kind of fear. In women's rooms, many users quietly scrutinize others heading into stalls to make certain they appear female enough. Women who look masculine often get a double take. And that little voice inside women's heads often asks: Is that a man, and could he be a sexual threat to me? US Department of Justice statistics suggest that only one in ten sexual assaults takes place away from the victim's home or the home of a friend, relative, or neighbour. But women, who experience the bulk of sexualized violence and who must be persistent and vigilant about safety in everyday places, worry, naturally, about sharing intimate space. That isn't the only reason behind women-only washrooms, of course: there is also the real, if demographically smaller, concern that members of certain ethnic and religious groups will stop going to public bathrooms if spaces are de-gendered. In conservative Islamic and Orthodox Jewish traditions, strict segregation between men and women is maintained. So, on the surface, it seems simple: women need women-only bathrooms. Men can stick to the men's.

But separate male and female public bathrooms are a minefield for trans and gender-nonconforming people, precisely because they are spaces where gender is rigidly enforced and where fitting in is limited to one of two options: you pick the door with the skirt or you pick the one with the trousers. Not only that. Users must then prove themselves worthy of using their chosen space to the strangers waiting inside. They have to pass. Trans and gender-nonconforming people who don't appear to fit the norms of male or female can be denied access. Sometimes it's by the managers of bars or restaurants, sometimes it's by security, sometimes it's by other users. The ways they are excluded range from innocent direction to the 'right' room to harassment and public shaming over entering the 'wrong' one. They can face threats and experience violence. Jody L. Herman, a public policy analyst at the UCLA School of Law, completed a 2013 study on the impact of gendered bathrooms on trans men and trans women. It reports that 68 percent of those surveyed had experienced verbal harassment in public restrooms at least once. Nine percent reported physical assault.

Enxuga says the potential for violence is one thing – acute and scary – but the underlying stress of not feeling like bathrooms are made for you is something else – lingering and damaging. Herman's study found that 54 percent of respondents reported physical problems from holding urine to avoid public bathrooms, including kidney and urinary tract infections. Cybelle Rieber, a former Pride Health coordinator for the Nova Scotia Health Authority, says she knows of people walking seven blocks from their place of work at the hospital just to pee in a single-stall gender-free bathroom. 'Bottom line,' she says, 'it's a health issue, let alone a mental health issue.'

It's also an impasse.

Many women who fear assault or who have been the victims of sexual violence maintain that multi-user bathrooms must continue to be gendered. But for trans and gender-nonconforming folks, divided bathrooms present the threat of violence and every-day dehumanization. For them, bathrooms shouldn't be places of gender compliance. They should be spots where anyone who needs to go ought to be able to go. No genders, no questions asked. The solution seems obvious from either side. And, I admit, I flit between the poles on this one. As a progressive, whose go-to is respecting people's experiences and their ideas for fixes, I want gender separation in bathrooms done away with. And as a woman, I can see the other side, too – sometimes I want space away from cis men. Just for a bit.

The gendered status quo of public bathrooms pits legitimate concerns against legitimate concerns. One way or the other, someone's need is being privileged and someone else's is being pushed down a peg.

A little defining, before we get any further: cisgender, or cis, describes a person whose gender identity matches their physical sex. I'm cis, because I have female genitalia and my gender is female, too. The opposite of cis is transgender, or trans. Trans describes a person whose gender doesn't match the one they were assigned at birth. So, a trans woman might have been born with a penis, but know she is a woman. A trans man may develop breasts, sure, but he's definitely a man. Or someone may not fit into either of the tidy binary gender categories. Someone who doesn't feel especially male or female, or who feels distinctly both, or neither: they are gender-nonconforming. Gender-nonconformity is often confused with being lesbian, gay, bisexual, or asexual – like the classic slur 'dyke' being used to describe a woman who doesn't appear feminine enough, or a little boy who doesn't like stereotypical male activities being called 'faggot.'

The questions trans men and trans women and gender-noncon-forming people who need to pee in public ask themselves are ones cisgender folks rarely wonder about: Am I going to get stared down? Am I going to get yelled at? In that context, bathrooms that seem perfectly accessible to the cis population may not be so easy to navigate after all. That's why Enxuga and a friend, Jake Feldman, came up with the Gender Neutral Bathroom Challenge in 2012. It was easy stuff: the two were sitting around talking one night about the bathroom frustrations they faced as trans men. They whipped up a Facebook page daring friends to use only gender-free bathrooms for one month. (Another common term is *all-gender* bathrooms; I prefer *gender-free* because, to my mind, when we talk about these bathrooms, what we're aiming for is inclusivity by not labelling gender at all.) Seven hundred people took them up on the challenge. He and Feldman wanted to raise consciousness, Enxuga says; they didn't want participants to come away from the month thinking they knew what it was like to be trans. 'It was to highlight how certain bodies and certain identities cannot occupy spaces that are often considered accessible,' says Enxuga. 'I think it's also interesting to think about bathrooms and why they are even gendered in the first place.'

Bathrooms most everywhere in North America and Europe are split down binary lines. Men in one place; women in another. This strict gender segregation even applies in many places where there are two side-by-side single-stall bathrooms. 'I was camping in the summer in the Yukon,' says Enxuga, 'and in the middle of nowhere they had two porta-potties. One for men. One for women. Why?' The simple answer: it's what we know. And opposition to change has proven, in recent years, to be vociferous. These arguments are of a different tone and texture than the long-standing point that some women feel safer in single-gender spaces. These messages aren't about balancing diverse needs. Them are highly politicized fightin' words.

In 2014, for example, reality TV star Michelle Duggar voiced a pre-recorded robocall that went out to residents of Arkansas, warning them of a bill before Fayetteville City Council that would allow people to choose bathrooms based on their gender identity. She urged Arkansans to fight the bill because, she said, having it pass would allow 'males with past child predator convictions that claim they are female to have a legal right to enter private areas that are reserved for women and girls.' Similar arguments about the dangers of male sexual predators dogged a November 2015 referendum in Houston, Texas, on Proposition One, which, had it passed, would have imposed fines of up to $5,000 on business owners who prevented anyone from using the restroom that matched their gender identity. Bruce Springsteen cancelled a 2016 concert in Greensboro to protest North Carolina's passage of a bill denying the rights of trans people to use the restrooms that matched their gender. And a debate raged all through the fall of 2015 over the rights of a seven-year-old transgender girl in Edmonton, Alberta's Catholic school system. The girl was asked by teachers to use her elementary's gender-free single-stall bathroom instead of the girls' bathroom, which she preferred. During a heated public meeting, one board trustee called being transgender a mental disorder. The family filed a human rights complaint.

There's no sign these issues will cool. Accepted North American numbers suggest the adult trans population is somewhere around .5 percent. Based on wait-lists for assessments for hormone therapy and referrals for gender-affirming surgery, that number appears to be rising. Despite great opposition, de-gendering public bathrooms will continue to be on the political agenda.

Enxuga would like to see more multi-stall gender-free bathrooms – where anyone can enter and use the facilities. But he concedes that for now it's culturally out of reach. I mean, we can't even all agree yet that a single-room toilet-and-sink public bathroom should be available to anyone. But he and I talked about another solution that straddles our society's competing desires for gender-free and single-gender spaces. I think of it as the 'three floors up' fix. And it's this: Enxuga and another activist ran a workshop once at which they made all the bathrooms on the main floor of the conference space gender-free. Anyone who wanted a gendered bathroom could go to the third floor. Like: 'You want a women's room? It's down the hall, around the corner, and up three flights.'

Bathrooms have long been policed spaces. Not only in the sense of gender being parsed and held up as pass or fail – but literally so. The 'morality squads' of police forces in major US and Canadian cities amped up their campaigns against sex between men, specifically, in the late nineteenth century, coinciding with the rise of public bathrooms. Of course, sex between men in public spaces was by no means new. In a world where gay behaviour historically has been frowned upon, men have long been forced to find space for sexual encounters where their families, friends, and community members would not discover them. Whether married or single, upper- and middle-class men could handily arrange private places for sexual encounters. Working-class men, on the other hand, have had fewer means for such safe seclusion. In his essay 'Through a Hole in the Lavatory Wall,' social historian Steven Maynard writes, 'For both lower-middle-class and working-class men the presence of a landlady or the hustle and bustle of a crowded working-class household meant that sex often had to be found outside the confines of the household, in the lanes and lavatories of the city.' After dark in public parks, these men weren't likely to stumble upon their mothers, wives, or co-workers.

The late nineteenth and early twentieth centuries saw an insatiable zeal for curbing 'immoral' behaviour. These campaigners, Maynard argues, saw stopping public sex between men as part of the general movement to halt the incursion of sex into popular culture in general. A community effort. But families couldn't forever keep a check on men seeking sex in parks, lanes, and bathrooms. So formal policing filled in. Maynard notes that in 1886, Staff-Inspector David Archibald of the Toronto Police's morality squad viewed the arrest of men having sex with men as a priority of his department. It wasn't just a pet project. The following year, Toronto's Markets and Health Committee made a formal recommendation to city council directing beat police to inspect urinals multiple times daily. That encounters may have been adult and consensual was not the point. And, with the introduction of 'gross indecency' to the Criminal Code of Canada in 1892, making a number of legislatively undefined sexual acts illegal, even a sex act's private or public nature became irrelevant.

The policing of sexuality in public spaces evolved, into the twentieth century, to include the surveillance of gender itself in public spaces. Aaron Devor and Nicholas Matte, in a 2004 essay about tension between gay and lesbian activists and trans activists, put forth a compelling theory as to why gender became so mixed up with sexuality in the policing of public bathrooms: 'It becomes considerably harder to delineate who is gay and who is lesbian when it is not clear who is a male or a man and who is a female or a woman.' What's consistent in the scrutiny of sexuality and the scrutiny of gender is how it's all undertaken in the name of safety. The common argument goes like this: allowing anyone who identifies as a woman into a women's bathroom means predatory cis men can call themselves female, enter freely, and sexually assault so-called 'legitimate' cis women. In a TV advertisement supporting the 'no' side of that Houston Proposition One referendum I mentioned, a hulking man in a multi-stall public bathroom pushes into a toilet stall behind a surprised and terrified little girl. The message is clear – the direct by-product of allowing anyone who *says* they're a woman into female bathrooms is that women and little girls will be raped.

Laura Shepherd remembers being 'hugely self-conscious and nervous as hell.' It was back in the days that Shepherd, a trans woman who grew up outside Lawrence, Massachusetts, was dressing as a woman only part-time. She would go to a shopping mall on a Saturday afternoon, like folks do, and, eventually, she'd have to pee, like folks do. Teenage girls would call her out in the bathroom in loud and demeaning terms. 'A middle-aged guy in drag walks into the washroom,' Shepherd says, 'and they all scream and run away. And I can hear them yakking from a distance. And then I see the same group ten minutes later when I am getting a coffee and they point.' Enxuga says he has never had this happen in a bathroom because he's a trans man. 'I am pretty privileged. I know people who suffer from more harassment, and they are trans women.' Shepherd agrees trans women have a harder time. Jody L. Herman's 2013 study, too, shows that the rate of verbal harassment is lower for trans men than for trans women.

Shepherd and Enxuga attribute this to trans misogyny: just as cis women are less valued in society and more open to criticism, judgment, and harassment, so, too, are trans women. But there are layers. Shepherd says trans men generally pass as men more easily than trans women pass as women. Plus, in Enxuga's words, 'men generally don't look at you when you are in the bathroom.' Every man I've asked about this agrees. It's eyes ahead, no talking – which gets back to that ingrained straight-guy fear of public bathrooms as sites of gay desire. Make too much small talk in the men's room and it's an invitation to or implication of something much, much deeper. This is a completely different experience than I typically have with the women – friends or strangers – I share public bathrooms with. We smile at each other. We make small talk. It's quite intentional.

Shepherd says her own bathroom habits have been influenced deeply by the almost half-century she spent using the bathroom with men. 'I use the women's room, but I use it like a guy. I walk in, I don't interact with anybody. I use it, I flush, I wash my hands, I get the fuck out. That's what guys do. I have never gone to the washroom with a friend. I have never had the opportunity.' Despite feeling like she doesn't always pass – 'I assume I look like a guy in a dress,' she says, though sitting across from her in a coffee shop, I beg to differ – Shepherd says her situation in public bathrooms is better now than before she began to transition. She says teenaged girls are still the hardest users to share with and she still gets dirty looks. 'It's not "Creep!" like it used to be. But it's not okay, either. It's not: "She is one of us." It's: "We have got to let her use this washroom."' Shepherd says women twenty to forty are informed enough to get it, but they don't talk to her the way they seem to talk to each other. By her own admission, though, Shepherd doesn't talk to them either. And what about her peers? (Shepherd is in her late fifties.) 'Heterosexual, cisgender women my own age?' she says. 'It's hard to know whether it's pity or respect, but there is a gentleness, either way. They will smile.'

So far in this chapter we've talked about two kinds of gender-free public bathrooms: the zenith of genderless sharing, the multi-stall; and the spacious single room with a toilet and sink with no gender labels on the door. Gender-free single-stalls are, on the face of it, pretty non-controversial. After all, they're what we all have at home. Gender-free single-stalls can be found outside the mayor's office at Boston City Hall and in the White House. Ontario's Ottawa-Carleton District Public School Board has them in its schools. So does the Vancouver School Board. The City of Portland designated six hundred of its existing single-stall bathrooms gender-free in 2016. The same year, Seattle passed an ordinance requiring existing and newly built single-stalls in all public places to be gender-free. West Hollywood City Council did the same a year earlier.

There is a whole range of reasons people might need a gender-free bathroom, and right up there on the list are children and adults who have opposite-gender caregivers. My friend Jen uses a wheelchair because of severe multiple sclerosis. Her caregiver is male. When he needs to empty the bag that collects her urine and there isn't a gender-free option, she heads into the men's room with him. She doesn't enjoy the impropriety, but she also doesn't really have a choice, except the option of having her caregiver come into the women's. 'I find guys are less freaked out,' she says. Gabriel Enxuga commits a similarly unrelished transgression when he uses a family bathroom – those single-room toilets found in many malls, with signage indicating they're for children and caregivers – as a stand-in for a simple gender-free one. Often, there are parents with kids waiting outside when he finishes. 'Because I pass [as male], I just look like an asshole using the washroom. It's not fair to me and it's not fair to other people.'

Even where the case for de-gendering single-room bathrooms is accepted, the appropriate signage can be a challenge. The Nova Scotia Health Authority installed 185 new signs on its one-stall hospital and clinic bathrooms in 2012. The signs show the traditional male and female stick figures – plus a half-male, half-female version below them. Cybelle Rieber, who was in charge of the change, says the response has been, for the most part, positive. But some trans and gender-nonconforming users don't like the new signs. The response from some of the community, says Rieber, has been, 'Why you are creating a third gender?'

Rieber says the health authority didn't choose the stick figures blindly. Researchers completed a scan of universal bathroom signs and consulted with user groups. They decided the phrases 'all-gender' or 'gender-free' would cause uncertainty for some people. 'Like, imagine you have a couple in their seventies,' says Rieber, 'and one is in the hospital for a heart attack and the other is there waiting to see how they are doing. And they have to go to the bathroom and they can't figure out the sign. That is the last thing we want to do – create an environment that makes people confused and that would cause stress.'

A straight-up toilet icon is the representation of choice for Portland's gender-free toilet initiative (showing, in the city's communications parlance, not 'who's allowed in,' but 'what's behind the door'). But the Nova Scotia Health Authority reasoned the toilet symbol wouldn't help some of the newcomer populations it serves, because toilets look different in different countries. The most common international symbol? Stick figures, according to Rieber. (I did wonder if they'd considered the smiling poop emoji, though I didn't tell Rieber that.)

That we are still grappling with the logistics of sharing space even when we are alone in single-user bathrooms is a clear hint that when it comes to the next evolution of gender-free bathrooms, the multi-stall variety, we just aren't there yet. There are success stories: New York's Whitney Museum of American Art, in 2014, began temporarily relabelling its lower-gallery multi-user restrooms gender-free for some events. Miraloma Elementary School in San Francisco phased out gender in its one-room kindergarten and first-grade classroom bathrooms in 2015 and has since converted most of the remainder of the school's restrooms, including its multiple stalls, to gender-free. But these are outliers in the world of gender conversion. Multi-stall de-gendering, in the US, mostly skulks along in the realm of heated proposition ballots like Houston's, and so far, the idea has been mostly shot down. But some public bathroom users, fed up with waiting, are taking matters into their own hands.

Sophie Massey is tentative about talking to me at first. 'But I've graduated,' she concedes, 'so it's okay to say this.' She's tying her shoes, getting ready for work, telling me about October 2013 at Wesleyan University. Massey and some friends, all of them students at the Middletown, Connecticut, liberal arts college, had begun a quiet campaign of tearing down male and female bathroom signs and replacing them with taped-up gender-free signs and, in some cases, a copy of the 'Desegregate Wesleyan Bathrooms' manifesto. The half-page statement called for an end to bathroom gender segregation in all campus buildings. 'We resent statements by Wesleyan Administration,' it read in part, 'that all-gender bathrooms are widely available on this campus, when they are in fact often difficult to find or unmarked, in inconvenient locations, or simply not available.' The letter was signed 'Pissed Off Trans* People' (they used the asterisk to denote trans as an umbrella term for all trans and gender-nonconforming people). The gender-free bathroom signs – one with an accessible symbol, another without, to fit the bathrooms where they were being posted – and the manifesto were available as a free online download. The zip file that landed on your desktop was called the Bathroom Renaming Kit.

Massey's friend wrote the manifesto. She is a trans woman for whom, Massey says, using the gendered public bathrooms at Wesleyan ranged from uncomfortable to unsafe. In the men's, 'she would get harassed. And she doesn't identify as a man. And using the women's bathroom, she gets dirty looks.' Massey, who asked me to use a female pronoun and who is, herself, gender-nonconforming, feels most comfortable in gender-free bathrooms

– 'less self-conscious and more free to express myself.' Back in 2013, she and others were upset with what they characterized as the slow movement of the university in setting up more gender-free bathrooms. A particular sore point was the school's Olin Memorial Library, which had no gender-free bathrooms. 'We had met with the dean,' Massey says, 'and he said, "Oh, I was supposed to get that dealt with over the summer, but I forgot."'

Massey and company's renegade campaign to de-gender Wesleyan bathrooms began that fall. In the campus athletic centre, the offending single-gender signs – plastic and glued on – came right off. A friend of Massey's carried around a screwdriver in her backpack for quicker sign removal. Which was convenient, it turned out, because some signs were wooden and took more work to wrench off. 'I was nervous someone would see me,' Massey remembers. They would replace the signs with paper gender-free versions. '[I felt] pretty good after.' Massey is funny and frenetic. 'Hang on,' she says, as she bolts up from our conversation and walks toward a corner of her living room, then back around, peering here and there. 'Where are they? I have them here. I have a bunch of the signs.' She presents a smattering of them – some chipped from their forced removal, some merely scraped; a couple made of wood, most plastic, all with either the traditional male and female stick figures or the words 'Men' or 'Women.' Several are adorned with the Wesleyan shield – a white, scallop-decorated cross on a red background, adapted by the university from the family coat of arms of John Wesley, the founder of Methodism. 'I have a shit-ton of bathroom signs here,' Massey says. 'Initially I had them on my [apartment] wall and I thought, probably not a good idea.'

Massey graduated in the spring of 2015 from Wesleyan. The school has an enrollment of fewer than three thousand students and is known for its open-mindedness. Massey figured, back in

2013, that what she and her friends were doing wasn't a big deal: 'I stole an American flag one time. I have done things worse than this and I just didn't think there was anything to worry about.' Until October 15.

Massey and another student got up in front of their Queer Anthropology class and made an announcement about the bathroom de-gendering campaign, encouraging students to join and, in effect, publicly outing themselves as central sign-removers. Later, she and four friends went to the Usdan University Center, Wesleyan's main activity hub, to remove more signs. Massey worked there part-time and she was seen by her boss, who confronted her. While the other students walked away, Massey told her boss she was frustrated with Wesleyan's lack of gender-free bathrooms and didn't regret her actions. The gang of friends returned and everyone engaged in a conversation about the de-gendering campaign with Massey's boss. The next day, she got a call to report to Wesleyan's Office of Public Safety to answer for her vandalism.

Mariama Eversley was a senior at Wesleyan when Pissed Off Trans* People started their campaign. She says it galvanized students, both for and against de-gendering. 'I started off being a little like, "I don't know if I want to share bathrooms with men,"' she says. 'And I changed.' Eversley says the group's action made a big impact because it was direct. Pissed Off Trans* People and their supporters were done talking about better bathrooms. Done listening to the administration talk about better bathrooms. They weren't interested in more delays or more debates. Eversley says, 'They just decided to go ahead and say, "You know what? We can do you a favour and make you gender-neutral bathrooms by taking down the signs and putting up a new sign."' She compares that kind of direct action with other successful campaigns that have brought simmering political exchanges to a boil. She mentions Bree Newsome, the North Carolina filmmaker and activist who was arrested in June 2015 for scaling the nine-metre flagpole outside the South Carolina State House and removing the Confederate flag, a long-controversial symbol of racism (or Southern pride, depending on your take). At a debate the following month, the state's general assembly voted to permanently remove the symbol of the Confederate states from the grounds. Since the debate had been planned well before Newsome yanked down that flag, we can't know if her actions had an effect on the vote. What's certain: she directly amped up the conversation on a contentious American social issue.

Did the actions of Pissed Off Trans* People help or hurt the cause of de-gendering bathrooms at Wesleyan University? Or, another way of putting that question: is it better to yank people out of their comfort zones with quick-and-dirty direct action or is an easy-does-it approach a better way to achieve lasting social change? Cybelle Rieber, reflecting on the bathroom sign changes in Nova Scotia's hospitals, says she believes in 'massaging the system.' Indeed: the health authority has only de-gendered one of its multi-stall bathrooms, and eleven buildings are still without any gender-free options at all. For Rieber, it's about 'gently changing the system so we can eventually get to radical change. But we can't get to radical change overnight.' But from Sophie Massey and her friends' point of view in 2013, overnight had come and gone, and still there was little evolution at Wesleyan. Mariama Eversley says students had asked repeatedly for more gender-free bathrooms, but the university had, in their view, kept taking advantage of the four-year student turnover to avoid dealing with the issue. Massey says she'd heard bathroom signs were being torn down for ten years before Pissed Off Trans* People acted. According to public and media relations manager Lauren Rubenstein, the university's approach all along was not to de-gender all multi-use bathrooms, but to work toward having at least one designated single-use, gender-free restroom in each academic and administrative building. Wesleyan is still working toward that goal; Rubenstein says the school added three or four new gender-free bathrooms in the 2017–18 academic year through a combination of renovations and redesignations. A school resource page lists fifty-six single-stall gender-free bathrooms. Fourteen buildings on campus are still without a gender-free option.

While Massey and the others may accuse Wesleyan of foot-dragging, the administration *did* respond to quickly to the 2013 de-gendering campaign. There was a disciplinary hearing in December to determine a punishment for Massey and two other students of the five at Usdan that October day. The remaining two came forward during the hearing. Some two hundred Bathroom Renaming Kits had been downloaded by then, but the university could only identify Massey and the Usdan crew. At one point, the total damage was assessed at $11,000. A letter of support for the charged students had been signed by four hundred alumni. At the disciplinary hearing, thirty community and campus activists were massed, ready to disrupt the proceedings, but Massey and the others called them off. After four hours of talking and testimony, the Usdan five were fined $450 – less than $100 each – which the students could pay in cash or by working for the university.

Massey was the only student to work off her fine. It was a particularly stinging job: reinstalling bathroom signs. Eversley calls the university's response heavy-handed. Wesleyan is known as 'Diversity University,' a place where liberalism is entrenched. It has a relatively open approach to gender and sexual orientation, including the 'Open House' LGBTTQQFAGPBDSM dorm. That's Lesbian, Gay, Bisexual, Transgender, Transsexual, Queer, Questioning, Flexual, Asexual, Genderfuck, Polyamorous, Bondage/

Discipline, Dominance/Submission, Sadism/Masochism. Some other on-campus residences include multi-stall gender-free bathrooms and showers. But Eversley says the administration used its response to the Pissed Off Trans* People campaign to send a message: 'You are not going to be deviant, and you are not going to be super-queer and weird in Usdan, where people who are going to give us money are going to come.'

The campus debate was heated, and well-publicized, partly because of national media attention, and partly because of a campus forum put on by a group called Wesleyan Diversity Education Facilitators (WesDEF). Eversley was part of this group, which sought to provide space to talk about the issues, rather than to choose sides. As the sign-jacking campaign had progressed, opposition to the de-gendering had solidified around women's fear of sexual assault. That was expected; in the Pissed Off Trans* People's manifesto, organizers had included a paragraph acknowledging that women, particularly, may feel unsafe in de-gendered bathrooms. 'We invite further discussion about this issue,' it read, 'but are currently not aware of any studies suggesting women are more likely to experience harassment or harm in all-gender bathrooms.' (I've never found any either, despite this argument being the go-to for anti-gender-free campaigners.) The debate came to a head at the WesDEF forum. In Eversley's retelling, 'A lot of cis women were like: "I have been assaulted. This is scary for me." And then there were genderqueer people who were like: "You are living in your comfort zone and you have no idea what my life is like. I don't have any bathroom I can go to, unless it's single-use."' Eversley believes women's very real fears, combined with the myth that most sexual assaults are perpetrated by strangers, kept many on campus from supporting Massey and the others. 'We are living in a situation where a lot of us getting assaulted is a reality. But in a bathroom? Not very likely. Probably at the party you are going to go to later. And not a stranger. Probably somebody you know.' US statistics show that 82 percent of sexual assaults and 80 percent of rapes are committed by someone known to the victim. Still, Massey admits, 'I don't think we took the things survivors of sexual assault were saying as seriously as we could. I think their concerns were dismissed.'

And that's the trick – finding a solution that doesn't leave anyone out, and doesn't put anyone at more of a disadvantage than they already are. Maybe it's Enxuga's third-floor-up solution. Maybe it's Rieber's fix – de-gendering only single-stalls in an effort to gently bring change. Maybe it's something else. And if not – if the competing, legitimate needs of cis women and of the trans and gender-nonconforming populations are simply unalignable – then what a limited scope of human ingenuity we must be dealing with. It's just sad. 'People talk about these ideas – about gender-neutral bathrooms – as if people have never thought through some of the logistical questions,' says Todd McCallum, a history professor at Dalhousie University who specializes in gender and sexuality. He likens today's discussions about gender to the way people bristled about accessibility changes for the physically disabled in the mid-twentieth century. To make space for all genders, he says, we will have to reconfigure bathrooms *and* the way we think about them. 'I imagine there is some system that allows us to go to gender-neutral washrooms, but that allows people, for whatever reason, including reasons of past trauma, to get a sense of safety they require. Will it cost money? Yes. But I just imagine this is easier to fix any number of other problems.'

As Eversley recalls it, that fall of 2013 was a 'battle period' at Wesleyan. The administration would remove the printed-off gender-free signs and duct-tape up new male and female signs. Then students would come by and rip those down, de-gendering the re-gendered bathrooms. There was never a clear sense among students whether the bathrooms were gendered or not, and many people just stuck to the spaces they knew. 'It showed us how disciplined we had become in going to the bathroom,' Eversley says; students were never able to really explore the feeling of sharing space. The spaces changed temporarily, but, to McCallum's point, they never got enough time living with the change to reconfigure their *thinking*.

Wesleyan's Olin Memorial Library, where only gendered bathrooms had existed before the 2013 gender-mutiny campaign, opened a new gender-free bathroom in July 2014. The ground-floor single stall was created by removing the shared wall between an adjacent storage room and custodial closet to form a brand-new single-use gender-free accessible bathroom. Massey smiles at this. She and the others didn't want costly new bathrooms built, only new labels. But while creating equality by jimmying off signs may be the cheap fix, as with so many of our public bathroom predicaments, it's not really about the cash.

As Gabriel Enxuga says, 'Our society isn't there.'

10

PIPE DREAMS

Brian Dean was making his slow, deliberate way along the sidewalk in Levenshulme, England, just outside Manchester, looking for a place to use the bathroom. The seventy-five-year-old had been out with his wife and full-time caregiver, Joan. The Deans had spent that January 2016 day in the seaside town of Blackpool, celebrating their wedding anniversary, and they were heading home to Stalybridge.

The stop in Levenshulme wasn't on their itinerary. But Brian has Parkinson's disease. Urinary incontinence and overactivity are common symptoms, and Brian had to go. The bathroom on the coach was too difficult to manage because of his condition, so they stepped off on Stockport Road in Levenshulme and looked around. No bathrooms. No signs. Brian tried a corner store, then a payday loan place. Next a Krispy Fried Chicken takeout, then a Subway restaurant. Finally, outside Subway, Brian wet himself in the street. Luckily, their son lived nearby in Manchester, and Brian called and asked him to leave work and bring him dry clothes so he and Joan could take their bus home.

Brian and Joan's saga made headlines all over the UK. What helped boost the story was that the Deans willingly became the face of the problem of disappearing public bathrooms and inadequate access in shops and restaurants. It's a rare man who pees his trousers on the sidewalk and is confident enough to stand up and declare the obvious: the problem isn't his body, it's the lack of access to toilets.

By the time I sit down to chat with Raymond Martin, the head of the British Toilet Association (BTA), he has already spent the day doing interviews about Brian Dean's saga. He tells me Dean's story. Then he repeats part of it, looking me straight in the eye, as if to underscore what I've just heard: 'He absolutely wet himself in the street.' The thing is, Brian Dean isn't a one-off. Martin receives letters every week from people who won't leave their homes because they know their own acute toilet needs, know there aren't enough public options, and don't want to pee their pants on a main street in front of a sandwich shop. For Martin, Dean's story underscores a simple truth – the matter of providing and maintaining public bathrooms must be taken on in a deliberate way – not just in Northern Ireland, where he lives, or in Levenshulme, or Stalybridge, or Manchester, but all around the world. And right now.

The BTA is a small association – it's only Martin and his 'right-hand man' daughter. But it's unflinching in its defence of the right to public bathroom provision. Martin calls the BTA linebackers for public bathrooms; its sister organization, the Loo of the Year Awards, he calls the cheerleaders: 'We are the guys who do the dirty work, and they are the ones who stand on the side and say, "You're doing great."' Martin has been a professional loo line-backer since 2000, but he's been preoccupied by public bathroom standards since the mid-eighties, when he became a widower with a newborn and a one-year-old. 'For the next ten years, my life was all around toilets,' he says. 'When we went into shops, or on holiday, or to beaches, I had to find toilets where I could take my girls.' Except, mostly, he couldn't. 'Men's toilets were revolting,' he says. 'We have managed to get the standards up quite considerably, we think, over thirty years. But you certainly couldn't take girls into men's toilets and I certainly couldn't go into ladies' toilets.' Martin's mother came to live with him early on, to help care for the girls, but she was diagnosed with cancer, and he then had the added challenge of finding facilities she could easily use as she got sicker. Toilets, Martin says, are 'in my psyche.'

Cities abound in toilets; not a building goes up without several. But, as we've seen, access is selective. Brian Dean was 'waved away' from the corner store he approached first. According to a story in the *Daily Mirror*, the workers who were behind the counter that day don't remember anyone asking to use the bathroom and, the manager told the paper, it was out of order, anyway. No word on where the actual employees were peeing that day, though I doubt they were wetting themselves on the street. The payday loan business couldn't allow non-employees into the back for security reasons. The two restaurant bathrooms were for customers only.

It might surprise you that Raymond Martin isn't pushing for retail businesses to open up backrooms to people coming in off the streets. He says there are legitimate reasons small businesses can't or don't allow people to use employee bathrooms. He doesn't even have harsh words for the customers-only cop-out. Martin has another solution: like Robert Brubaker, his counterpart in the American Restroom Association, Martin believes that providing bathrooms should be the business of government. Not merely the responsibility of spacious and well-off big retailers, and not the burden of small shops, but routine political practice. Problem is, he says, 'the government doesn't see public toilets as a political issue.' And so, public bathrooms don't have a stand-alone departmental home in the UK, nor in many other North American jurisdictions. Researching this book, I have dealt with parks and recreation officials, water commissioners, planners, development officers, and others. I've never heard tell of a public bathroom department or office. Like a retrofitted main-floor powder room squished into what was once a coat closet, toilets get wedged in where they get wedged in. In the UK, the US, and Canada, their existence is not mandated, and there's no money automatically earmarked for them that funnels down the chain of government to the villages, towns, and cities that are on the front line of residents' toilet demands – and their sometimes inevitable toilet emergencies.

On top of that, funds to councils are, on trend, decreasing. In 2011, just before a rash of public bathroom closures, local council budgets in the UK were cut by 23 percent. Mostly, the reductions ended up hitting discretionary services – nice-to-haves rather than must-haves. Councils have to clean the streets, collect the garbage, and keep up the cemeteries. But they don't have to put up flower boxes. They don't have to install basketball courts and skateboard parks. And apparently they don't have to provide public bathrooms, which are one of the costliest so-called nice-to-haves around, once maintenance and utilities are tallied up. Add to that all the social challenges we've seen around public bathrooms – wheelchair access, gender and parity issues, and provision for the homeless, just for starters. Bathrooms are no piece of cake. You can't install them and forget them. So it's easier for councils to save the money and avoid the challenges and opt instead for closure. 'We were the envy for a long time because we had toilets everywhere,' says Martin. 'Suddenly, now we have a situation where councils have said, "We don't have to do it, there is no legislation, there is no regulation, we don't get any financial support – cut them."'

But public bathrooms are too important to be considered nice-to-haves. 'Toilets are about health and well-being, they are about equality, they are about social inclusion, and they are about public dignity and public decency,' Martin says. Without enough of them, the economies of small towns and independent businesses suffer as shoppers choose suburban malls over downtowns and village high streets. Tourism is affected. Street urination increases. But Martin doesn't even care if you buy all that. Toilets, above all, are about health, he says. 'Bladder and bowel and Alzheimer's – those things are on the rise no matter how much the charities are putting into them.' More people with more conditions and diseases means more bathroom need.

In June 2015, Wales health minister Mark Drakeford put forward a bill to, among other things, force local councils to provide a strategy for public bathroom provision. He wasn't necessarily asking them to install new facilities or dive into costly fixes for old and decrepit ones. He simply wanted every town and city council in Wales to set out a plan showing how the needs of the elderly, the sick, visitors, and others would be met. The draft law came after a 2012 Welsh National Assembly Health and Social Care Committee report that linked the existence of public bathrooms to better public health outcomes.

Martin tells me he applauds the move by Drakeford, in part because of its aim of forcing councils to start strategizing about public bathrooms rather than ignoring them. But mostly, Martin likes the wider political meaning in tying toilets to health. 'For the first time,' he says, 'toilets will have a home.' (Well, turns out they won't, actually, because since I talked to Martin, the bill's been defeated. So much for that, then.)

While forcing local councils to think more about toilets has hit a brick wall in Wales, in New York, one toilet – nickname: Bob – was thought about perhaps a little too much.

Bob was the pet name for an installation at Columbia University, a joint project between masters students in the School of the Arts and the Graduate School of Architecture, Planning and Preservation. Bob was an outdoor pavilion comprising a stage and seating area, a bar, and a projection screen. Oh, and an inflatable white canopy, filled by way of the off-gas from a public toilet. Bob was the site of screenings and events all through the summer of 2011, while the canopy, like a gaseous cloud, loomed overhead. Okay, okay – in reality, it was filled by a fan, not farts. (I mean, how many farts would it take to fill a ten-metre cloud?) But we'll get to that part of the story in a moment.

The pavilion, and particularly its toilet component, was inspired by a 1990 statement by conceptual artist Carl Andre in the *Journal of Contemporary Art*. Here's what he said: 'A society which cannot afford clean, attended public facilities does not deserve public art.' Adrian Coleman is on board with Andre's notion. 'Society should provide basic infrastructure for the people,' says Coleman, who was one of the architecture students who designed and championed Bob. 'Public bathrooms are part of that infrastructure, the same way roads and other things are. And if you can't even get that right, how can we go further? That's the starting point, basically.'

The Columbia campus spans more than six blocks in Morningside Heights, just north of Manhattan's Upper West Side. The grounds and buildings bleed into the fabric of the city; it's hard to tell, in some places, whether you're on campus or if, by walking down the sidewalk, you've slipped into the city proper. But if someone arrives on campus looking for a bathroom, and they aren't a student or faculty member with the right ID, there's no way that person is getting access to the can. The Bob team knew this, and interpreted it as elitism. 'It was kind of revealing, the invisible walls that existed, but that you couldn't actually see,' Coleman says.

Galia Solomonoff, the Bob project's faculty advisor, was the one who originally brought the Andre quotation to the group. She says the university sits in a middle zone. 'Things seem public,' she says, 'but when you dig under the surface a little bit, you see they are not. Whether you want to take out a book to read, or go to a class, or use the phone, or take a nap, or do anything.' So, the group wondered: what would happen if we plopped a public toilet down smack dab in the middle of a Columbia courtyard? How would that change that middle-ground dynamic? How would that challenge the elitism? How would that point to the bigger social issue – the school's failure to help meet a basic human need? The group was about to put the rubber to the road when it came to Carl Andre's stance. It was about to find out if Columbia deserves public art.

The initial plan was to plumb in a toilet behind a projection screen: the person using the bathroom would be unseen by the folks watching whatever was being shown on the screen but would themselves be able to see what was being projected. They quickly realized there was no simple way to bring water and sewer pipes to the middle of the courtyard. No problem. Bob would have a composting toilet, which breaks down human waste through decomposition. In fact, Bob would *be* the composting toilet – the bathroom soon became the focal point of the pavilion, and the design group began referring to the toilet itself as Bob. They started working on the design, budgeting for construction, and ordering materials. The giant inflatable cloud 'fart' balloon had to be specially made in China. Because, apparently, you can actually have *anything* made in China.

Work chugged along, until Columbia's facilities management department told the students they could only use the toilet for display. No one was going to be allowed to use it to relieve themselves. By Coleman's telling, and that of fellow architecture student Shai Fuller, the Columbia response was, generally, nervousness. They were worried about health concerns, leaks. The students also weren't allowed to put a door on the toilet enclosure because that made it 'a place where people could get trapped,' Coleman says, 'where there was no visibility.' Fuller puts it this way: 'There was an element-of-shock factor that we were going for, and I think that was difficult for them. It's like: let's have people go to the bathroom in the middle of our beautiful courtyard. You know, homeless people. It's not an easy thing to say yes to, for them. So many things in their minds could go wrong. And it's also not the most refined thing. It's messy – socially and physically.'

Even with no working toilet, they still had the fart balloon and they still had to make it float. In came the fan. Coleman says outside people visiting the pavilion reacted most to that big balloon. (No doubt – the images are striking; it's a massive white canopy that looks like an upside-down, mid-air bouncy castle.) People were drawn to the composting toilet, too, but more out of curiosity about its environmental, rather than social, impact. 'We didn't really think of it as a sustainability project. We thought of it as a democratic project,' says Coleman. Solomonoff says it's a shame the metaphorical meaning of Bob – which centred on access – was a little lost. Plumbing, in general, and public bathrooms, specifically, have helped make urbanism viable, she points out. Plumbing must be organized 'so a density of people can get together. If not, we could not live the way we do. It's enabled a city like New York to grow.'

As it happens, Bob the toilet lives on today, in a garden. A second home, Fuller calls it. Bob is no longer a missed metaphor for enforced elitism, but a real, live working bathroom in a community garden in the Bushwick neighbourhood of Brooklyn – 'not the hip part of Bushwick,' Fuller says. 'Very low income.' The Bob team donated the toilet and Fuller designed the enclosure for it – half bathroom, half storage. In fact, there were no public bathrooms close to the garden in this section of Bushwick. Before Bob arrived, the caretaker had been relieving himself in a shed.

When you gotta go, you gotta go. It's a truism perhaps somehow more true when it's two in the morning and a bar patron has been topped up by last call and unleashed on the urban environment.

This was architect Matthew Soules's challenge. Soules never imagined that designing a public urinal would be such a high point in his artistic career, but there it is: the Victoria Public Urinal in Victoria, BC. Not that toilets *can't* be art. Marcel Duchamp's famous 'readymade' work, *Fountain*, is a prefabricated urinal laid on its back, signed and dated 'R. Mutt 1917.' It's one of the central works of twentieth-century Dadaism. But there are functional works of bathroom art, too. There's the Trail Restroom outside Austin, Texas, designed by Miró Rivera Architects, which is a coil of steel plates leading to a spacious, gorgeously rugged bathroom cubicle. There are the Kumutoto public toilets on Queen's Wharf in Wellington, New Zealand, designed by Studio Pacific Architecture – a striking pair of headless brontosaurus-like shapes roaming the pier. (Apparently some people call them the 'lobster loos,' but all I see are dinosaurs, myself.) There are DnA Design and Architecture's public bathrooms at the Jinhua Architecture Park in Zhejiang Province, China – individual concrete periscopes rising up out of the grass.

For some people or, perhaps, people in some states of intoxication, peeing outside in the middle of the city is no biggie. That's a problem for many downtowns, leading to stinking streets, in the best cases, and damaged buildings, in the worst. Officials in Chester, England, asked late-night revellers in 2012 to please, *please*, stop peeing on the walls of the town's seven-hundred-year-old city-centre walkways. So much urine was being deposited when the clubs let out, the historic walls were being eaten away. Victoria's public pee problem wasn't as bad as that. But the city wanted to curb it. And it wanted to do so with a little flair.

The Victoria Public Urinal is in the tradition of nineteenth-century French pissoirs, which allowed screened, stand-up urination on city streets. But instead of ducking behind a little metal pissoir wall, Victoria Public Urinal users follow a spiral into the centre of the structure, where a standard fixture awaits. The urinal, which sits across the street from Victoria City Hall, is made up of 165 vertical steel pipes, which would look exactly like the kind used for street signs and parking meters were they not powder-coated green. The pipes are mounted in an undulating pattern – people on the outside can see if the urinal is in use, but not who's using it, and someone on the inside can see people approaching. It's private, without a door. Artful and useful. They didn't come up with a zinger name for it, but I suppose we'll forgive them that.

'How can we make this totally exciting and interesting?' That's how Michael Hill, Victoria's community development coordinator, says his team approached commissioning the urinal. Hill and his co-workers received several concept ideas – an origami urinal, a living-wall urinal. In another, patrons would have walked in and peed between two giant boulders. When Soules's ideas arrived, Hill says, 'we thought: this is who we want designing this thing.' The planner says this kind of beyond-the-pale project often doesn't happen in bigger cities, where the bureaucracy is a deeper and weedier river. 'We are small enough that we can talk amongst ourselves and we can get things done.' Hill also says Victoria is big enough to think big – to know the value of aesthetics. But the Victoria Public Urinal wasn't made to be strictly art. It was zoned-in, no-messing-around municipal problem-solving.

Street pee was big in Victoria in 2005 and 2006. Talk of the town. The downtown's alcoves and corners were awash and the stench was conspicuous. The street community was getting blamed. Hill wrote a report and found that, in fact, it was largely bar-goers, not the homeless, who were turning the streets into toilets. After the bars let out, he says, 'it's like a conveyor belt.' A 90-percent-male conveyor belt. (More on women's role in street-peeing in a wee bit.)

The first fix the city went for was a small weekend army of plastic portable urinals. They looked a little like inside-out porta-potties, with four spots to pee, one on each corner. They were trucked in at ten o'clock on Thursday, Friday, and Saturday nights and collected around three in the morning. The urinals were $1,200 each to buy and maintain, and moving costs were, at $7,000 annually, more than the city wanted to pay. The city decided to try again. Hill's team considered a Urilift. By day, these modern pissoirs stay hidden underground and look like oversized manhole covers. At night, they rise up out of the ground – slowly, plantlike. When the entire Urilift is above ground, it locks into place and is ready for use. Urilifts are popular in Europe, but the manufacturer wasn't enthusiastic about going through the process to attain Canadian Standards certification.

Hill and company kept looking, but nothing was perfect. 'Some are a little more sexy,' Hill says, 'but in every case we didn't feel like the designs were what we were looking for.' So they wrote a request for proposals and fired it off. Soules, a newly licenced architect, stumbled across the posting. 'You could see it was written intelligently and it could be good,' he says. The 'question of the design,' in Soules's words, was how to create a building that was deeply private and deeply public at the same time: 'Something that functions as a public urinal, where people from all walks of life feel comfortable using it at all times of day, and at the same time make it resistant to sex, drugs, vandalism, all that kind of stuff.'

Sex, drugs, and vandalism were the obsessions of Hill's team – they had been warned by stores and restaurants that the reason they'd closed their own washrooms to the public was that when they checked them, they'd often find blood and needles. Sometimes people would hole up and use sinks for sponge bathing, which, no matter how understanding you might be of the predicament of someone who finds himself or herself forced to bathe in a restaurant basin, is a big mess to clean up. Bathrooms would get trashed. So Soules's design couldn't use a door to achieve privacy. A passing police cruiser had to be able to see users' feet, in addition to a number of other criteria that would balance transparency and opacity. It had to fit the budget – $60,000 – and be ad-free, unique to Victoria, and able to be replicated across town. On top of everything, it had to be beautiful. 'In one sense, this is the most banal, quotidian thing,' Soules says. 'You go to architecture school because you dream of designing museums. But the fascinating thing was the higher ambitions they had.' The urinal was installed in 2009. It won the International Downtown Association's Pinnacle Award for public space. In the summer, people get their picture taken in front of it, laughing and high-fiving.

But there haven't been any more built.

It's not that they aren't needed. Sure, there are also long-standing public bathrooms at nearby Centennial Square. But those bathrooms have been intermittently closed due to drug use and drug dealing, and other issues (in Hill's big 2006 report on public bathrooms, he includes a photo from Centennial Square of a large pile of human feces on the floor in a corner). Today, the facilities are patrolled by security twenty-four hours a day. The city also has a second-generation late-night portable urinal program. This one is a three-way partnership between the city, a consortium of downtown bar owners, and Our Place, a local social services provider. The city bought the portable urinals (Polycans – they cost $250 each and look like little lidded trash cans) and the trike they are brought in on. Our Place delivers them to their locations and assigns staff members to clean and maintain them. And the bar owners pay for maintenance and transport. Hill says they know the program is working because they have feedback from private property owners and city crews that cleanups are down. Plus, one weekend, they didn't put the urinals out, to see what would happen. 'The guys came in and said, OH MY GOD. There was so much to clean up,' recalls Hill. Even with the portable program running well, the city started negotiations with Soules to bring more permanent urinals to the core. But first they had another issue to deal with: women.

Gender was very much a part of Soules's and Hill's urinal conversations from the get-go – should it be equally friendly to all? What they settled on was that the urinal was not a public amenity in the conventional sense. 'The pressing problem was not to provide a public good,' says Soules, 'even though [the city] wanted it to be aesthetically pleasing. They didn't want to provide a service but to calm that specific problem.' In short: men were known to be causing the woes, so the fix was tailored to target their behaviour. Here's the rub: 90 percent of errant pee-ers might be men, but women are still out there in the bars, still needing a place to go, and, in limited volume, still peeing in alcoves and urban cubbyholes. Recall George Bernard Shaw's recounting of the condition of St. Pancras's little byways and nooks. This is not a new problem. Victoria's women needed provision. Plus, the city's solicitor advised Hill that the city would likely face a Charter challenge if there were scores of male-only urinals popping up around downtown and nothing for women.

While the urinal fixture inside Soules's design is placed to allow women to hover over it, and has small handles to help women manoeuvre into position, 'whether any woman has actually done that,' Soules says, 'I don't know.'

Hill was undeterred. He launched a pilot project with female city staff, giving them a device called the P-Mate, which directs the flow of urine out and away from women's bodies. (Similar disposable and non-disposable devices are marketed under a variety of different brand names, such as Lady J, GoGirl, and pStyle – order online for all your portable peeing needs.) Hill sent his co-workers out with their P-Mates while he considered how the city would dispense them, whether it could contract a local box company to make them cheaper, and what kinds of City of Victoria messaging could be plastered on the side of these tiny portable penises. The results from Hill's co-workers were mixed. 'Some of them said, "Yeah, they work really well." Some of them said, "I'm not. I'm just not."' Whether the cultural shift needed to popularize the P-Mate was a challenge Hill was up to, the world will never know. The city's risk manager weighed in next. 'I will put it in my words,' Hill says. 'Basically, if something happened to a woman with her pants down inside one of these urinals, it would be like, *what*? What was the City of Victoria thinking, having a twenty-one-year-old drunk woman pulling down her pants outside, downtown, at two o'clock in the morning?'

The city worked with Soules to redesign the urinal as a toilet, producing some promising designs, but his urinal's simple balance of public and private was a pickle to reproduce. A toilet needs to be in a bathroom. A bathroom requires a door. A door meant a greater chance of sex, drugs, and vandalism.

The next downtown public convenience Victoria installed was a Portland Loo – the gender-free off-grid prefab bathroom that has found such success in other West Coast cities. The Loo isn't a beauty like Soules's urinal ('looks more like a utility kiosk from BC Hydro,' Hill says), but it gives everyone, at least, a spot to squat. And it, too, is a product of deeply ambitious thinking – both in the aspirational, community-involved way it has been implemented (as we've already seen), and in its simple, useful design.

The community development folks in Victoria, and the Portland Parks and Rec people – even, ultimately, Shai Fuller and Adrian Coleman and their art and architecture classmates at Columbia who built Bob – weren't relying on high concepts, but an on-the-ground truth: cities need toilets because people need toilets. But there's another, commensurate truth: those people and cities need toilets that *work*. This is fixer thinking, with a dash of creativity tossed in. As the BTA's Raymond Martin puts it: 'What we are saying is, there are options.' Victoria proves it. Portland proves it. And those cities prove a point, too: getting public bathrooms right takes not just thinking about them, but thinking about how to get them right.

EPEELOGUE

Rachel Erickson figured she'd be doing Shakespeare. Leading an animated walking tour of Bard-related landmarks around London, she guessed – the Globe Theatre, Southwark Cathedral, that kind of thing. Instead? 'People started paying me to talk about toilets.'

Erickson's story finds its genesis the way so many good stories do: with a bathroom tale. Erickson moved from Richmond, California, to London in 2012, to study theatre. As she explored her new city, she noticed that many UK public bathrooms cost money to use – thirty pence, sometimes fifty pence. 'The same as a chocolate bar!' she says. She launched a personal research project: collecting a list of cheap or free places to visit the can. 'I had this obsession.' (Heh. Yeah. Tell me about it.) Erickson happened to mention her peculiar mapping scheme to someone from the tour-guide company she had just signed on with. He suggested she plan out a toilet tour. 'How?' she asked him. 'We'll go and pee for three hours?' Not quite. But Erickson became the Loo Lady – taking people on tours of the high and low points of London public potties. On her walkabouts, she talks politics, history, and the nitty-gritty of London's grittiest and niftiest public bathrooms. She ends at a pub where tour-takers can continue their fun. 'Ten people who have never met each other before together in a pub telling their toilet stories,' she explains.

Well, of *course* they are. Erickson knows it. I know it: everyone's got a good bathroom yarn. I've spent a decade-plus pondering public bathrooms as a journalist; longer still pondering them as a mere bathroom-scouting human. From that way-back time when I peed in my velveteen trousers, waiting in line at the community hall dance while the next-over boys' room went unused – and even before then, surely, in ways I don't even remember – I have collected my own public bathroom stories. We all have. And in that sense, we're all public bathroom researchers, aren't we?

Rachel Erickson tailors her toilet tours to whomever shows up with a ticket. She once did a private run for the tenth birthday of a boy on the autism spectrum. He wanted to look at toilets and flush each one. She has done singles tours, in cahoots with an online dating company called DoingSomething, the premise being that a blind date is more fun when you're, um, doing something. 'I think they had a good time,' she says.' I mean, I have taken dates to sewage treatment plants.' (Be still, my toilet-adoring heart.) Sometimes her tours are hilarious and pun-filled, some-times they are more political. Always, they're crammed with facts. The Romans and their sponge-on-a-stick trick, Jennings and the Crystal Palace monkey closets. Crapper, Cummings, George Bernard Shaw – a roll call of all the usual suspects most folks have had their toileting lives influenced by, but about whom they probably know nothing. Most of her participants are Brits. After that, Australians and Americans. Oddly, only one Japanese tourist ever. Generally, she says, 'it does attract the kind of retired crowd who pine for the golden age of those beautiful Victorian toilets.'

Erickson graduated and her UK visa ran out, so she returned to California in 2014, leaving the tour business temporarily in the capable hands of three other loo obsessives: 'They are almost as enthusiastic about toilets as I am.' While she managed the London business from Richmond, a bedroom community near San Francisco, she started scoping out a version of the loo tour for the Bay Area. It was tricky. Though the rise of public amenities started around the same time in the US as it did in the UK, in the mid-nineteenth century, there was never that golden age of Victorian provision in places like California. 'Because we are much more of a driving culture,' she says, 'you find that there are toilets in the parking garages, in the highway rest stops. Not glamorous or exciting.' There's also, perhaps, a different approach in North America to the concept of on-street bathrooms. Erickson was out on a field study of potential Bay Area tour stops one day and while she was paused in front of a JCDecaux APT, a police car pulled up. 'The policeman said, "You don't want to go in there." And I was like, "Oh! Story!" He said, "Just use the café. You don't want to go in there."' Story indeed. I guess that was before the San Francisco Pit Stop program came into effect. Erickson also says she sees more and more restrooms near her home with 'Customers Only' signs. Couldn't that, I wonder, be part of the tour? Or maybe the divergence in toilet culture between the UK and the US is just too great to make Erickson's business work.

In the end, it's moot. Erickson moved back to London in 2017 and is still deep into loo touring. 'Brits take a bit of pleasure in toilet humour and talking about toilets,' she says. 'Americans don't always get it as quick.'

Erickson told me she became the Loo Lady 'by accident.' Now, how many times have I heard that? It's the same with 'Toilet Lady' Clara Greed, and with *Bathroom* author Barbara Penner. It's the feeling of Raymond Martin from the British Toilet Association and GottaGo! Ottawa's Joan Kuyek. It's my story, too. We all got stuck in, and we never got unstuck. My kids are older now – teenagers. Gone are the days when we tromped together down to those grim concrete stairs to yank on the handle of the Pavilion bathrooms on the Halifax Common. Now, even when we find ourselves on a busy downtown street with no public bathrooms, no one is at risk of an accident. They are more in control of their bodies, my girls. And, crucially, they are trained in their knowledge of the public bathroom landscape. They have learned, as all of us must, to hold it. As long as need be.

Beyond their enhanced understanding and control, not a whole lot else has changed. My city, and most others I've researched and visited, remains mired in its own toilet training – struggling to manage user needs and to recognize the toilet as a basic human right. There are some bright spots. Remember those plastic portable toilets I told you about, the ones the City of Halifax rented each winter for the 120,000 visitors to its new speed-skating oval? In the time it's taken me to write my way from the first chapter to this last, those porta-potties have been replaced. The oval now boasts a bricks-and-mortar building, including spacious bathrooms with rubberized flooring so skaters can walk in on their blades.

But if you've followed me this far on the journey, you know that public bathroom access isn't just about constructing rooms with toilets and sinks. It's about cultural access, too. *Any* old toilet isn't always the *right* toilet. There will still be many people, at many times, in many places, who will have no place to go. And that's why there are those of us who go beyond the role of everyday researcher – beyond just retelling our toilet tales over dinner or at the pub – to being public, political, and pushy.

More than thirty years after founding All Mod Cons, Susan Cunningham (another accidental loo lady) is still involved in toilet activism, well beyond being the official holder of the organization's boxes and folders and files. In 1999, the group merged with the Loo of the Year Awards to become the British Toilet Association, which Cunningham helmed for a time (now headed by 'linebacker' Raymond Martin). She still regularly cranks up her toilet volume. Writing letters, demanding better. She delivered a speech at a 2011 Welsh Senate of Older People 'P is for People rally' at the Welsh Parliament. At the time, the BTA estimated there were 40 percent fewer public bathrooms in the UK than there had been ten years before. The losses of loos have increased since. Raymond Martin estimates it's 50 percent now.

Mike Bone and his wife, Donna, run the Loo of the Year from their office between London and Brighton. The organization is contracted to inspect toilets in England, Scotland, Wales, and Ireland – ones in service stations, airports, shopping centres, or parks. The Loo of the Year measures one hundred different bathroom criteria, including 'Are the urinal outlets free from any debris – cigarette butts, litter, etc., and free from malodour?' and 'Is there a colostomy bag shelf available adjacent to the WC?' An inspector from the organization writes up a report, grading the facility, and the bathroom is entered into the awards. The Loo of the Year encompasses national and UK prizes in fifteen market sectors and an astonishing sixty-one categories, as well as certificates of excellence for attendants. In 2012, the Bones added platinum to the bronze-silver-gold grading system as a way to up the stakes and to commemorate the awards' twenty-fifth anniversary. That made 2017 its thirtieth anniversary. It's been going that long. The highest loo honour is the eponymous Loo of the Year Award, heralding the best of the best in public conveniences – a gold toilet-seat trophy, engraved with the names of past winners.

Bone came from a toilet background, working for years as the operations director for a company that provided commercial restroom services. He prizes clean public facilities – 'unless we have good toilets, everybody suffers,' he says – but just as much, he takes pride in being the guy who makes everyone want to improve their loos. 'Just knowing that you are satisfying a basic human need. We need to eat, we need to drink, we need friends, we go to the loo.' And who wouldn't want to be the purveyor of a shiny golden toilet-seat trophy, anyway?

'Urine is really where it's at, in terms of nutrient recycling, but shit is about the heart, and the soul, and the mind.'

Those are the words of Shawn Shafner. Or his alter ego, the Puru. To be honest, it's hard to tell them apart sometimes. Shafner is an actor, educator, and artist who founded the People's Own Organic Power Project. If your acronym synapses fire fast, you've already clued in that it's the POOP Project. Shafner runs classes and workshops, makes art, and, most notably, mounts stage shows that get people talking about their bodies and how they deal with what comes out of them.

As a child, Shafner had encopresis. With the condition, children, mostly, avoid defecating for days or weeks. As impacted feces fills the colon, it distends, allowing liquid stool to involuntarily escape around it. Over time, the stretched colon and rectum can suffer nerve damage, which dulls the sensation of needing to pass stool and can cause permanent fecal incontinence. Shafner was a child actor. He says holding his feces was a way of coping with other aspects of his childhood that felt out of control. He was skipping fourth grade, going to LA for pilot season, and being home-schooled so he could fit in auditions. 'I think there was this balance of, I'm an actor, I am so fancy, and I am shitting my pants and no one can know.'

By middle school, Shafner had improved, but during high school, he did a study-abroad in Spain and fell back into his old poop-holding habits. One night, after a two-week stretch of not defecating, and being at the point where he could no longer eat, he finally got the job done – promptly clogging his host family's toilet. Shafner went to his host mother, Maria Teresa: 'I know it's, like, midnight, but I have a problem,' he told her. 'I can't flush your toilet.' Maria Teresa took water from the sink and poured it over Shafner's turd until it would flush down. Then she told him what he already knew: 'This is why you've been having all those tummy aches. You need to poop every day.' No shame. 'I got compassion, and love, and kindness,' he says. 'It shifted. It was like: *boom*.'

After that, Shafner was on fire. He read up on poo. He researched the psychoanalytics of shit, the marketing of toilet products, the woeful state of global sanitation, and the concepts of 'clean' and 'dirty' and their meanings in broader culture. And he started to make art – songs and installations. And shows. *Eat $h*t* was at the Edinburgh Fringe Festival in 2012, a musical about the environmental cycle of human waste and how we aren't quite getting it right. *An Inconvenient Poop* came later. The latter is framed as a TED Talk gone wrong and covers Erasmus to etiquette, laying bare the Western plague of what Shafner calls 'fecal denial.' Like when we go to another floor of our office building to poo – and I'm not talking about Gabriel Enxuga's 'third-floor-up' solution here. Or when we buy sprays to hide the smell, like Poo-Pourri, whose tagline is 'Spritz the Bowl Before-You-Go and No One Else Will Ever Know!' What Shafner found, onstage in his 'I'm a Pooper!' T-shirt and afterward, talking to his audience, was the same thing Rachel Erickson discovered at her tour-end pub stops – everyone has a toilet story. 'They are like, "Oh, I have a cousin who…," "I have an aunt who…," "Have you ever been to this place?" "Have you seen this thing?"'

Shafner's shows include discussions of fecal transplants and Martin Luther's obsession with excrement. They inform audiences that the US House of Representatives didn't get a women's toilet near the floor until 2011. And that every twenty seconds a child dies from diarrhea. Informing through art is Shafner's way of being part of the solution. 'I am not a scientist and I am not an anthropologist and I am not an engineer,' he says. 'I'm not going to go build toilets in India.' Shafner was at the United Nations in 2013, speaking at the festivities on November 19 – World Toilet Day. Among weighty discussion of global sanitation and social justice, he urged those attending to remember toilet needs in the Western world, too, and he pressed people on the obligation to banish taboos. 'Culture-makers,' he told the assembly, 'are the next generation of people to take this on.' (One 'I'm a Pooper!' T-shirt at a time.)

Shafner becomes the Puru, practically, talking to me from his New York home office, books and art supplies behind him. I'm only sad that it has to be over Skype: I don't get the full, in-person Puru. 'Fart with fury. Poop with passion. Pee with pride,' he booms. Is this the spirit and enthusiasm we toilet researchers share? 'There is a little bit of a clan,' Shafner admits. 'You gotta be a little bit of a weirdo to latch on.'

Lucy Davey insists she does not have a fetish for toilets. But how else does she explain spending her free time driving up and down the Cornish coast of southwest England taking photos of public bathrooms?

Davey and a photographer pal, Karen Butfield, made a habit in 2014 of travelling the coast to shoot landscapes and sea cliffs. They would hop in a car from their homes in Par and Tregony, head to Newquay, and go for it down the seaside. Eventually, they'd be looking for a bathroom. 'I have had three children,' Davey says. 'I am going to have to wee.' But Cornish public bathrooms were few and far between. And fetid. 'We had a laugh and a joke, and said, "We should do it as a documentary,"' says Butfield.

So they started work on a photo book – tracing the tenacious hanging-on of the public johns they found, and making a point, too: 'Our toilets are being closed on a weekly basis,' Butfield says. 'In about ten years' time, the public toilet might be extinct.'

Davey shoots the exteriors in black and white; Butfield, the insides: 'A lot of colour and rather grotty.' Davey shows the architecture of each toilet and where the facility fits into the community surrounding it. Butfield has other insights. The accessible bathrooms have the most trash lying around. The women's have bits of toilet paper all over the floor. (Oh, believe me, *I* know.) The men's rooms stink to high heaven, but are, at least, tidy. 'Women spend more time in there,' Butfield says. I offer my theory – men don't use toilet paper or wash up as much. 'In a way, it's to show the public how disgusting humans can be,' Butfield says by way of a measured response. 'When we were out a few weeks ago, we met up with a couple of toilet cleaners from Newquay Town Council and we got talking to them and we were recording the photos to show what the cleaners have to deal with sometimes.'

Theirs is not an easily explainable art project. Butfield is sometimes caught exiting the men's bathroom with a camera and tripod. Or Davey will briefly stop people from accidentally walking into her shots. 'You say, "Hang on, I'm just making a social documentary." And they are like: "Wot?"' The general reaction, Butfield says, has been a microcosm of the larger conversation around public bathrooms in the West. 'You either get, "Oh that's disgusting!" and "Why!?" and "What a waste of time! Are you strange?" Or other people want to talk about it. They have experiences and ideas to share.'

Paul Talling is another UK photographer documenting the aesthetics of disappearing bathrooms – these ones in the urban core. His website, Derelict London, documents abandonment and ruin. He started out wanting to capture the misery of buildings with history and architectural allure being closed and falling into disrepair before being demolished and replaced by shadows of their former charming selves. Along the way, he ended up chronicling, in large number, the loss of on-street public loos.

Talling says most of the damage and decay happens after buildings are shuttered, not before, as if closure is a hastening toward inevitable demolition. 'The below-ground [bathrooms], which are grated off, accumulate street litter on the stairwells and encourage rats,' he says. In the ones that are not secured, 'you find a lot of syringes down there and there is the overpowering stench of where people have still used the toilets but not been able to flush.' It's a fact, I got to thinking, that you can close as many bathrooms as you like, but there are always going to be people about, and those people are always going to need to go somewhere. Talling calls public bathrooms in Britain 'an endangered species,' along with traditional pubs, cafés, public drinking fountains, and red telephone boxes. He, like the folks at the BTA, blames local councils, who have no legislative obligation to provide service and who know these city-centre sites are prime real estate. Two of the erstwhile public bathrooms he's shot have become a wine and charcuterie restaurant and a lunch bar, respectively. Another abandoned toilet – ironically, near the former site of Crystal Palace, where Jennings had his monkey closets – has been developed into an apartment building.

Talling documents a changing urban landscape. Not just the aesthetics, though. His photos mark a cultural shift, too. The dwindling number of public bathrooms represents the loss of a unique asset – one that is shared, intimate, and essential to the growth of cities. Urban density could not exist without public bathrooms. Cities themselves would become sick and die without interconnected sewage pipes to carry away human waste. I've come to an understanding writing this book: the story of public bathrooms is the story of cities; the shifts in their availability is a story of evolving urbanity. Shared solutions to human waste have existed as long as people have congregated. Ancient India, and Babylon, and Minoa gave way, in the West, to Rome and its aqueducts, to the Great Stink of 1858 London and Joseph Bazalgette's ensuing fix. To a golden age of public conveniences, to the cleaving away of that public provision and its replacement by commercial interests. What will give way next? Sewer systems in many major North American cities are cresting one hundred years-plus and need urgent work. Or maybe we're headed for another, different, golden age of public bathrooms. I used a composting toilet in deep rural Nova Scotia at an ice cream place a few years back. The woman taught me how to crank it when I was done. She did the same for the next person in line after me.

Have we ever granted toilets – and especially public toilets – their due? Have we given them credit for how they've helped grow our world? As gross or goofy or quotidian as they may seem, public toilets represent higher notions and beliefs. Fundamentally: who is in and who is out. Whom we see as part of the city. Whom we see as human. This book has been, I hope, a rallying cry. But not for clear-cut solutions to poor access. What I pine for is a different view altogether of the public bathroom. For open dialogue. We'll never make bathrooms better if all we do is recoil and titter and turn a blind eye. In my perfect world, public bathrooms don't get solved exactly. They get seen; they get talked about. They get feted.

My personal celebration? I don't carry little girls' underpants around with me anymore. But I'm old enough to look ahead to my own ineluctable slide into old age and think of how I, someday, will be where my kids were a decade and a half ago. Looking urgently for a place to go.

A Reading List

Katherine Ashenburg. *The Dirt on Clean: An Unsanitized History* (Alfred A. Knopf, 2007).

Bill Bryson. *At Home: A Short History of Private Life* (Doubleday, 2010).

Sheila Cavanagh. *Queering Bathrooms: Gender, Sexuality, and the Hygienic Imagination* (University of Toronto Press, 2010).

Susan Cunningham and Christine Norton. *Public In-Conveniences: Suggestions for Improvements* (The Continence Foundation, 1995).

Aaron H. Devor and Nicholas Matte. 'The Uneasy Collaboration of Gay and Trans Activism, 1964 –2003,' *GLQ: A Journal of Lesbian and Gay Studies* (2004).

Rose George. *The Big Necessity: The Unmentionable World of Human Waste and Why It Matters* (Metropolitan, 2008).

Aaron Gordon. 'Why Don't We Have Pay Toilets in America?' *Pacific Standard* (September 17, 2014).

Clara Greed. *Inclusive Urban Design: Public Toilets* (Architectural Press, 2003).

Peter Greenaway, director. *Inside Rooms: 26 Bathrooms, London & Oxford-shire* (1985).

Morna E. Gregory and Sian James. *Toilets of the World* (Merrell, 2009).

Stephen Halliday. *The Great Stink of London: Sir Joseph Bazalgette and the Cleansing of the Victorian Metropolis* (Sutton, 2001).

Jody L. Herman. 'Gendered Restrooms and Minority Stress: The Public Regulation of Gender and Its Impact on Transgender People's Lives,' *Journal of Public Management & Social Policy* (Spring 2013).

Alexander Kira. *The Bathroom,* Revised edition (Penguin, 1976).

Lucinda Lambton. *Temples of Convenience & Chambers of Delight* (History Press, 2007).

Steven Maynard. 'Through a Hole in the Lavatory Wall: Homosexual Subcultures, Police Surveillance, and the Dialectics of Discovery, Toronto, 1890–1930,' *Journal of the History of Sexuality* (October 1994).

Harvey Molotch and Laura Norén, eds. *Toilet: Public Restrooms and the Politics of Sharing* (New York University Press, 2010).

Barbara Penner. *Bathroom* (Reaktion, 2013).

——. 'Researching Female Public Toilets: Gendered Spaces, Disciplinary Limits,' *Journal of International Women's Studies* (June 2005).

——. 'A World of Unmentionable Suffering: Women's Public Conveniences in Victorian London,' *Journal of Design History* (2001).

Fran Reiter. 'The Agony of Public Policy Making: New York's Quest for Public Toilets,' independent study project submitted to the Marxe School of Public and International Affairs, cuny/Baruch College (October 2005).

George Bernard Shaw. 'The Unmentionable Case for Women's Suffrage,' *Englishwoman* (March 1909).

David Waltner-Toews. *The Origin of Feces: What Excrement Tells Us About Evolution, Ecology, and a Sustainable Society* (ecw, 2013).

Nick Watts, director. *The Toilet: An Unspoken History* (2012).

Bathroom Renaming Kit: http://www.mediafire.com/file/wx5e49 fmvj49rrb/Bathroom+Renaming+Kit.zip

The Great British Public Toilet Map: https://greatbritishpublictoilet map.rca.ac.uk

The Charles Booth's London Archives, London School of Economics and Political Science: https://booth.lse.ac.uk/map/16/-0.0978/ 51.5112/100/0

'Progress on Drinking Water, Sanitation and Hygiene,' 2017 Update: https://www.unicef.org/publications/files/Progress_ on_Drinking_ Water_Sanitation_and_Hygiene_2017.pdf

'An Urgent Need: The State of London's Public Toilets' (Greater London Authority, March 2006): https://www.london.gov.uk/ sites/default/ files/gla_migrate_files_destination/archives/assembly-reports-health-public-toilets.pdf

Acknowledgements

It took me two years to write *No Place To Go*. But really, it's taken my whole life, learning and relearning the cultural place of public bathrooms.

My research comprised a dog's breakfast of materials – interviews, field visits, published and unpublished academic writing, and no small amount of time spent scouring daily papers from all over Canada, the US, and the UK. Much of my fact-finding involved the simple detailing of tiny moments in people's larger lives – their struggles finding adequate provision, their workarounds navigating public spaces. Bathroom stories are often the narratives, as a society, we cannot share. And I am indebted to those who did.

I am grateful, too, for the supporters who kept me upright during this work. *No Place To Go* is a direct product of the Master of Fine Arts in Creative Nonfiction program at the University of King's College, where I was guided by my mentors, Tim Falconer and the indomitable Kim Pittaway. Thanks to King's Stephen Kimber for the nudge, and to Don Sedgwick, for telling me to write about public bathrooms for my MFA and not those other things, whatever they were.

Great swaths of this book were written in libraries, which are the greatest places in any city, besides, of course, good public toilets. Patricia L. Chalmers, like all first-rate librarians, became engrossed during my early research. Two Arts Nova Scotia juries awarded me funding to keep this work going. CBC Radio's Christina Harnett has been a friend and professional booster, and was the first person who encouraged me to keep on the toilet beat.

Thanks to Simon Thibault and Ian Roy for unwavering gentle encouragement. Thanks to Andrea Dorfman for being my long-time professional and personal sounding board, and Dave Hayden, who is a beautiful human I am grateful to know I can always count on. Thanks to Christine Oreskovich, for her enduring best-friendship, and Kyle Shaw, who came up with the title for this book, and practically every pun in it. Thanks to Sarah Cook for love (and chocolates) sent across an ocean, to the enduring Catherine Stockhausen, and to Renée Hartleib for solving all my problems. Thanks to Elaine Flaherty for warning me to never accidentally type 'pubic' when I mean 'public.'

Thanks to my mother-in-law, Joanne Ritchie, for doing whatever, whenever, and always knowing to do it before anyone even asks. Thanks to my father, Richard Lowe, who, helpfully, always asked: 'What's the next step?'

Thank you to Anita Chong, who deserves *all* the sharp pencils; Carolyn Forde, my agent at Westwood Creative Artists; and Alana Wilcox, editorial director at Coach House Books – you all believed in a book about public bathrooms, because you are patently awesome. Melanie Little, my manuscript editor, saved me from myself a thousand times over. (Really, you have *no idea*.)

Thanks, most, to Kevin Lewis, Lily Lowe, and Georgia Lewis, who put up with me, and all this non-stop public bathroom this-and-that. You three are loved even more than my favourite public bathrooms.

Lezlie Lowe began her freelance radio, newspaper, and magazine career in 1996. She has penned and produced long-form pieces on urban rats, roadkill cemeteries, sex work, and, prominently, public toilets. She has made a writing career out of flipping on the lights above society's unexamined everyday. Lowe has been a finalist and multiple winner at the Radio Television Digital News Association Awards, the Atlantic Journalism Awards, and the Canadian Association of Journalists Awards. Her job as principal researcher helped win the Atlantic Film Festival Rex Tasker Award for Best Documentary for *Sluts: The Documentary*. Lowe has taught journalism at the University of King's College since 2003.

Since her first news magazine piece on public bathrooms appeared in 2005, Lowe has written extensively about the design and accessibility of these unsung facets of urban development. She blogs about municipal amenities at lezlielowe.com and has gathered a posse of fellow public toilet scrutinizers on Twitter @lezlielowe.

Typeset in Whitman and Gotham.

Printed at the Coach House on bpNichol Lane in Toronto, Ontario, on Zephyr Antique Laid paper, which was manufactured, acid-free, in Saint-Jérôme, Quebec, from second-growth forests. This book was printed with vegetable-based ink on a 1973 Heidelberg KORD offset litho press. Its pages were folded on a Baumfolder, gathered by hand, bound on a Sulby Auto-Minabinda, and trimmed on a Polar single-knife cutter.

Seen through the press by Alana Wilcox
Edited by Melanie Little
Cover design by Ingrid Paulson
Author photo by Riley Smith

Coach House Books
80 bpNichol Lane
Toronto ON M5S 3J4
Canada

416 979 2217
800 367 6360

mail@chbooks.com
www.chbooks.com